TURNING **POINTS**

TURNING POINTS

Preeminent writers offering fresh, personal
perspectives on the defining events of our time

Published Titles

William Least Heat-Moon, *Columbus in the Americas*

Scott Simon, *Jackie Robinson and
the Integration of Baseball*

Alan Dershowitz, *America Declares Independence*

Thomas Fleming, *The Louisiana Purchase*

Eleanor Clift, *Founding Sisters and
the Nineteenth Amendment*

William F. Buckley, Jr., *The Fall of the Berlin Wall*

Martin Goldsmith, *The Beatles Come to America*

Forthcoming Titles

Bob Edwards on Edward R. Murrow and
the Birth of Broadcast Journalism

Sir Martin Gilbert on D-Day

Douglas Brinkley on the March on Washington

Kweisi Mfume on Abraham Lincoln and
the Emancipation Proclamation

The Beatles
Come to
America

Also by Martin Goldsmith

The Inextinguishable Symphony: A True Story of Music and Love in Nazi Germany

TURNING POINTS

The Beatles Come to America

MARTIN GOLDSMITH

John Wiley & Sons, Inc.

Published by John Wiley & Sons, Inc., Hoboken, New Jersey
Published simultaneously in Canada

Design and production by Navta Associates, Inc.

For general information about our other products and services, please contact our Customer Care Department within the United States at (800) 762-2974, outside the United
States at (317) 572-3993 or fax (317) 572-4002.

Wiley also publishes its books in a variety of electronic formats. Some content that
appears in print may not be available in electronic books. For more information about
Wiley products, visit our web site at www.wiley.com.

Library of Congress Cataloging-in-Publication Data:

Goldsmith, Martin, date.
   The Beatles come to America / Martin Goldsmith
      p.   cm.—(Turning points in history)
Includes bibliographical references (p.) and index.
   ISBN 0-471-46964-5 (alk. paper)
  1. Beatles. 2. Rock musicians—England—Biography. 3. Rock
music—Social aspects. I. Title. II. Turning points (John Wiley & Sons)

ML421.B4 G64 2004
782.42166'092'2—dc22   2003021222

Printed in the United States of America

10 9 8 7 6 5 4 3 2 1

For Amy

Bliss was it in that dawn to be alive,
But to be young was very heaven!
                    —WILLIAM WORDSWORTH

Contents

1. Forever 1
2. "Genius Is Pain" 7
3. A Flaming Pie 27
4. Laboratory and Conservatory 43
5. The Toppermost of the Poppermost 61
6. "O Come All Ye Faithful,
   Yeah, Yeah, Yeah!" 85
7. "Such a Feeling" 101
8. "The Beatles Are Coming!" 115
9. "A Vision of the Ecstasy of Life" 129
10. The Children of Bishop Martin 167

Acknowledgments 185

Select Bibliography and Videography 187

Index 189

1

Forever

There are places we remember all our lives.

On a soft English summer evening at peaceful twilight, I stand before an ornate gate, its iron bars painted bright red, that connects two high stone pillars. Trees whisper overhead, and birds sing their welcome to the oncoming night. Through eyes wide with wonder and smeared with happy tears I read the words on the pillars: *Strawberry Field*. I have never been here before. But oh, how I remember this place!

It is today, as it was in the 1950s when a boy named John Lennon would come around the corner to attend band concerts, a girls' orphanage run by the Salvation Army. The rambling Victorian mansion that once commanded the grounds has been replaced by a functional but prosaic series of flats. Strolling through the grounds, I come upon a swing set and a sandbox, a single shoe, a soccer ball, and an abandoned teddy bear. I stoop to pick up the bear, and as I straighten, a movement above me catches my eye: a little girl waves to me from a window. I smile and wave back, and feel indescribably happy.

I have come to Liverpool, tracing a mighty river to a sweet spring bubbling up from the depths of the earth, trying to understand the dark mystery of creation as I seek the source of the undying magic of the Beatles. Over three days I visit homes and schools and churches, a subterranean club called the Cavern, and a suburban street called Penny Lane. Each of them is ordinary, and yet each appears to me suffused with the warm glow of memory. They are places I seem to have known all my life.

Earlier in the day, standing on the banks of the river Mersey as its swift current flows north to the Irish Sea, I think of Fitzgerald as I, too, am "borne back ceaselessly into the past." Today the Beatles, the act we've known for all these years, are about as big as they've ever been, their newly remastered CDs and DVDs selling in the millions worldwide. But for me and for so many others of my generation, the Beatles occupy a vital place in our past. Two places, really—the place we met them, and the place that prepared us for that meeting.

On Friday, November 22, 1963, President John F. Kennedy was assassinated in Dallas. Even those who questioned the accomplishments of his Thousand Days in office felt the immediate and profound loss of Kennedy's youth, wit, and style. On the following Monday, November 25, the President's body was buried at the conclusion of a riveting and solemn funeral procession. That national day of mourning was marked in the minds of millions who tuned in via television by the numbing tattoo of muffled drums that accompanied the flag-draped caisson through the streets of Washington, D.C., on its way to Arlington National Cemetery. It was a day for tears, not for music.

Seventy-six days later, on Sunday, February 9, 1964, millions of Americans once more gathered around their televisions to witness another turning point, this time in the cultural history of the country. Four musicians from Liverpool, all in their early twenties, performed live on *The Ed Sullivan Show* and helped dispel the gloom of that death in November. The arrival of the Beatles in America, and the two weeks they spent on these shores, unleashed unbridled joy and unparalleled excitement in an emerging generation and brought about lasting changes in music, broadcasting, journalism, and fashion, and in how that new generation saw itself and the world around it. The heart of the Beatles' enormous impact was their music, but its sinews were made up of the boys' youth, wit, and style. What had been so violently lost was now found again.

Ask most Americans who are now between the ages of fifty and sixty where they were on those two dates— November 22, 1963, and February 9, 1964—and they will be able to tell you with overwhelming certitude. Those days are places we remember all our lives.

Since it's television that linked those two events so profoundly, it is interesting to recall that Newton Minow, the man President Kennedy appointed to head the Federal Communications Commission, once famously condemned TV as a "vast wasteland." Minow was referring to one of the most famous poems of the twentieth century, *The Waste Land* by T. S. Eliot, a meditation on modern-day alienation that in turn was partly inspired by the Grail legend, the medieval romance of the Fisher King, and the exploits of the Arthurian knight Percival. In the legend, the king has been gravely wounded and the crops of the surrounding lands have withered and died. It is only through the intervention of the knight that the king's country is restored to health.

Is it giving the Beatles too much credit, forty years later, to imagine them coming to our wounded country in its time of trouble, wearing their Arthurian haircuts and singing their songs of love and joy—taking a sad song and making it better—and restoring our emotional health and happiness? As someone who believes deeply in the power of art to make individuals whole, I don't think so. What works for a single soul works for a nation.

There is, after all, something mythical and deeply romantic about the Beatles. Their creation, how the teenage John Lennon and Paul McCartney happened to meet on a summer evening in 1957, is the stuff of myth, as is their journey to the underworld of Hamburg, where they summoned the strength that enabled them to conquer the world and reign supreme as gods of music until, after ten short years, they passed into immortality.

One of the greatest of the Romantic poets, Percy Bysshe Shelley, declared that poets and artists are "the unacknowledged legislators of the world." The Beatles were supreme artists who contributed a singular voice to an eloquent generation. They supplied hope and wonder and an unquenchable optimism to an age that, at its best, believed deeply in the perfectibility of humankind. As the decade deepened and their music grew ever richer in melody and message, the unwavering arc of the Beatles' accomplishment provided an artistic parallel to the great scientific venture of the era, and one of President Kennedy's signal challenges, the journey to the moon. Most important, and from the very beginning, whether we screamed out our pleasure or just sat entranced, the Beatles brought us joy, a feeling comparable, as John Updike told me, to "the sun coming up on Easter morning"—endlessly renewable and life-affirming.

The sun has now set over Strawberry Field this summer night. Somewhere overhead a blackbird sings. As I make ready to leave the red iron gate, a car pulls up and a man and a woman emerge with a camera and walk toward me. Their slightly dazed and uncomprehending expressions no doubt mirror my own of a few minutes ago. They begin to speak quietly to each other, and I recognize a few words of Russian; they, too, have come from far away.

We three stand silently for a time, looking at the words on the pillars. Then the man turns to me and says, haltingly, "Please . . . you take picture?" I nod and take the camera, and, once they have arranged themselves properly in front of the gate, I engage the flash and snap off three shots. They bow and come forward to retrieve their camera.

Clearly awed, the woman whispers wonderingly, "Strawberry Fields!" I nod again, smiling, and suddenly the three of us are locked in a warm embrace, faces aglow, deeply happy at our shared pilgrimage and our memories of a timeless music. We slowly disengage, they start to walk away, and then the man turns back and adds softly, ". . . forever!"

I watch their car roll away, and then, with a singing heart, I begin to trudge up the hill through the gloaming toward a certain church where it all began.

2

"Genius Is Pain"

The village of Woolton will never be confused with Vienna or London or Memphis as a major center of music. But it was there in the summer of 1957 that two of the most creative musicians of the twentieth century met and began their magnificent partnership. The anniversary of July 6, 1957, ought to be celebrated every year with fireworks and dancing—and, of course, great rock 'n' roll. On that Saturday afternoon, in St. Peter's Church Field, John Lennon met Paul McCartney.

The occasion was the Woolton Village Fete. If you drive through England's green and pleasant land during the summertime, virtually every town and hamlet you come to will display hand-lettered signs announcing the time and place for its fete—what we in America would call a fair. There are parades and animal displays and food and drink . . . and musical entertainment. The English pronounce this French word as if it were spelled "fate"—which in the case of the Woolton Village Fete of 1957 is highly appropriate. Including when Mozart met da Ponte and Rodgers met Hammerstein, I can think of no more fateful meeting in the history of music.

Woolton is a suburb of Liverpool, that sprawling seagoing metropolis of the north of England, a city that received its initial charter from King John in 1207 and from which the first great ocean liners of the Cunard Line set forth in 1840. The city is named for the liver bird, and its emblem is a pair of green copper cormorants holding bits of seaweed in their beaks, presiding over the city from their perches atop the Royal Liver Building down at the city dock, the Pier Head. The celebrated writer and humanist Matthew Arnold lived in Liverpool, the German composer Max Bruch conducted the Royal Liverpool Philharmonic during the 1880s, and the notorious (and fictional) Fanny Hill was born there. So, too, were all four Beatles, and it is that fact alone, more than all the Cunard steamships that ever sailed, that has spread Liverpool's fame to the ends of the earth.

As a busy port city and a major supply line during World War II, Liverpool was a natural target for the German Luftwaffe. Beginning with the Battle of Britain in 1940 and continuing for more than three years, the city absorbed an almost nightly pounding from the air. A grim joke that made the rounds of Liverpool's pubs declared that you could walk across the river Mersey, which separates the city from the county of Cheshire, by stepping on the blasted hulls of sunken ships.

The Beatles all came into the world during that violent period in Liverpool's history. Paul lyrically recalled his birth in a couplet he wrote for his *Liverpool Oratorio* in

1988: "The air-raid siren slices through/The air in 1942." It was June 18, 1942, to be exact, when James Paul McCartney was born in a private ward of Walton Hospital in Liverpool. His mother, Mary (immortalized years later in "Let It Be"), was a nurse and midwife. His father, Jim McCartney, was a cotton salesman who, in 1942, was too old for active duty in the war but served as a firefighter, helping to put out blazes started by the German bombs.

Paul remembers the aftereffects of the war very well. "We played on bomb-sites a lot," he recalls, "and I grew up thinking the word 'bomb-site' almost meant 'playground.' I never connected it with bombing. 'Where are you going to play?' 'I'm going down the bombie.'"

Paul's brother, Michael, was born in 1944, and the family began to move around what Paul called the "frontiers" of Liverpool: suburban villages named Anfield, Wallasey, Speke, and Allerton. As a practicing midwife, Mary would be transferred from one area to another, where she would look after all the expecting mothers and receive free housing as part of her compensation. But despite all the moving about, Paul remembers a very warm, very loving home life. His extended family included a couple of uncles—Jack and Harry—and two aunts—Milly and Jinnie—to whom he was very close. He told me a few years ago, on the occasion of the American premiere of his oratorio *Standing Stone*, that he learned a great deal about simple human kindness from his aunts. "I've met presidents and prime ministers, but no one I've ever met has had the ability my aunties had to talk to me, give me a cup of tea, and find out exactly what was wrong."

Paul also credits his family with giving him musical genes. Jim McCartney played the piano at home and, as a younger man, had played the trumpet in a jazz ensemble called Jim Mac's Band—a group that also featured Paul's Uncle Jack on trombone. Jim was self-taught as a musician and apparently passed on that ability to his older son; Paul took a few piano lessons as a boy but didn't like them (his piano teacher's house "smelled of old people"), and he never learned to read or write music. But he has some tender childhood memories of lying on the floor and listening to his father play the piano. "He was my musical education," Paul says.

But the turning point in Paul's life as a musician involved his mother. The family had recently moved to a snug little house at 20 Forthlin Road in Allerton—Paul had just turned fourteen—when Mary began to experience pains in her breast. She was forty-five years old and decided that the pains must have something to do with the onset of menopause. So she ignored them for several weeks until they became unbearable and she forced herself to see a specialist. He diagnosed breast cancer and sent her to Liverpool's Northern Hospital for emergency surgery. Sadly, the treatment came too late, and only hours after the operation she was dead.

Jim was devastated. Paul did his best to soldier on. "My mother's death broke my dad up," he remembers. "That was the worst thing for me, hearing my dad cry. I'd never heard him cry before. But I was determined not to let it affect me. I learned to put a shell around me at that age."

The shell apparently had a musical core. Paul's Uncle

Jack had given him a trumpet and encouraged him to follow Jim's example. Paul managed to pick out a few tunes but was never passionate about the instrument. But then, right after Mary's death, at least according to his brother, Michael, Paul became obsessed by music. "It took over his whole life. You lose a mother—and you find a guitar? I don't know." What we do know is that Paul bought a guitar for fifteen pounds and began to play.

What makes a successful musical partnership? There are probably as many answers to that question as to what makes another sort of artistic alliance, a marriage, successful. In my experience, similarities attract. And in the phenomenal musical partnership that was Paul McCartney and John Lennon, there were many important similarities: of background, temperament, tastes in music. But there was also one overriding difference between the two, a difference that seemingly was the anvil against which their distinctive natures were dashed, producing the sparks of their inspiration: Paul was fundamentally a happy, contented soul, and John was forever haunted by sadness and anger stemming from his earliest days.

"When I used to talk to John about his childhood," says Paul, "I realized that mine was so much warmer." John, in an interview after the Beatles broke up, said, "My mother and father split when I was four and I lived with an auntie. The worst pain is that of not being wanted, of realising your parents do not need you in the way you need them. I was never really wanted. This lack of love went into my eyes and into my mind. The only reason I am a star is because of my repression. Nothing would have driven me through all that if I was 'normal.'"

John's father, Fred Lennon, was a man without moorings, brought up in an orphanage and later employed as a waiter on several of Liverpool's Cunard liners. In photographs, he looks like one of those eager, seedy characters who are usually played to perfection by Michael Caine. John's mother, Julia Stanley, the youngest of five sisters, met Fred by chance in a Liverpool park just days after he'd left the orphanage. For more than ten years the two saw each other during Fred's leaves from the sea. Fred's father, Jack Lennon, had spent many years in America as a professional singer, performing with a group called the Kentucky Minstrels. His one legacy to his son was a banjo, and during Fred and Julia's decade-long courtship the two would play banjo and sing together.

On a cold day in December 1938, they got married, on the spur of the moment and as something of a joke. Julia was working as an usherette at the Trocadero Cinema in Liverpool, and they spent their honeymoon watching films from the plush red seats of the "Troc," laughing and kissing and eating sweets. When the last feature was over and the projector went dark, Fred walked home to his place and Julia took the bus to hers. The next day Fred resumed his job as a ship's waiter and sailed off to the West Indies for three months.

On October 9, 1940, during a thundering air raid, Julia delivered a baby boy at Liverpool's Maternity Hospital. Perhaps because, four months earlier, she had heard her prime minister declare defiantly that "we shall never sur-render," Julia named her son John Winston Lennon. Fred was off at sea.

Julia moved back in with her parents. For the next eighteen months her only communication from Fred was the child support payments that he sent from wherever his ship life took him. Then, with no warning, the payments stopped. Julia, assuming that Fred had abandoned her, began seeing another man and parked her son with her older sister Mary Elizabeth (known as Mimi) and Mimi's husband, George Toogood Smith, who owned a dairy. They lived in a smart semidetached house at 251 Menlove Avenue in Woolton. Little John began to think of Mimi and George as his parents.

When John was not quite five years old, Fred Lennon suddenly reappeared in Liverpool with a fantastic tale of how he'd gotten drunk in New York, spent time in jail—first on Ellis Island and later in Africa—and then, during the arduous journey back to England, made "bags of money" selling black-market stockings and other contra-band. Fred asked if he could take John with him on a trip to Blackpool, a famously threadbare English seaside resort, to get acquainted. Both Mimi and Julia gave their approval, and off the two Lennons went.

Had matters gone the way Fred intended, the world might never have heard of either John Lennon or the Beatles. Fred had a friend in Blackpool who had already made arrangements for the three of them to pull up stakes in England and start their lives over down under in New Zealand. But just before their ship was due to sail,

Julia turned up in Blackpool to demand the return of her son. The two adults argued for hours, and when they couldn't resolve the dispute, they turned to John and, in a variation of the story of Solomon, asked the baby to cut himself in half by choosing which parent he wanted to live with. John chose Fred, but after watching his mother walk away, he ran down the road after her, crying. Julia picked him up and carried him back to Liverpool.

But not to live with her. John went back to Menlove Avenue to live permanently with his Aunt Mimi and Uncle George. Mimi and George had no other children and did nothing to dissuade the neighbors of the idea that John was theirs. They kept a neat house and a neat little garden, growing gooseberries, blackberries, raspberries, and currants in the summertime, and paying John an allowance of five shillings a week to mow the lawn. He remembered a strict upbringing with few outings. The family attended the occasional Walt Disney film, the Christmas show at Liverpool's Empire Theater, and, every summer, a carnival—featuring a Salvation Army band—that took place at a former Victorian mansion, now a girls' orphanage, just around the corner from Menlove Avenue. The mansion was on the site of an old farm that used to grow strawberries; its name was Strawberry Field.

John developed a rich inner life during his years at Mimi's house. There were books to read—Oscar Wilde, Kenneth Grahame, and Lewis Carroll were his favorite authors. "I was passionate about *Alice in Wonderland* and drew all the characters. I did poems in the style of the 'Jabberwocky.' I used to love Alice and *Just William*. I loved *Wind in the Willows*." In the back garden of the house on Menlove Avenue was an immense elm tree, and John would often disappear up into its branches for hours on end, dreaming and drawing and writing down poems.

Those years and those places were a vital source of inspiration for John's most famous work. Strawberry Field in particular seems to have been his Rosebud, a cherished image from the past that stayed with him always. A line from his greatest autobiographical song, "Strawberry Fields Forever," takes on a new resonance when you think of the boy in his leafy hiding place: "No one I think is in my tree. . . ."

And he learned from the people around him. "There were five women that were my family. Five strong, intelligent, beautiful women, five sisters. One happened to be my mother. Those women were fantastic. The men were invisible. I was always with the women. They always knew what was going on. That was my first feminist education."

Fred soon became only a distant memory, but Julia remained a presence in John's life. Mimi told him that she lived far, far away. In fact, she lived only a few miles from Menlove Avenue and dropped in from time to time. Once she appeared with a bruised and bleeding face, having been struck by her new lover. John fled into the garden. "I couldn't face it. I thought, that's my mother in there, bleeding. I loved her, but I didn't want to get involved. I suppose I was a moral coward. I wanted to hide all feelings."

But if John Lennon tried to hide his true feelings from the world, he did little to mask what seems to have been the dominant emotion of his youth: anger. He began to get into fights at his first school, Dovedale Primary. He shoplifted, first swiping candy and apples from open-air markets in a nearby street called Penny Lane, later making some easy money by stealing and then selling cigarettes.

"I was the kingpin of my age group," John remembered. "The sort of gang I led went in for things like thieving and pulling girls' knickers down. When the bomb fell and everyone got caught, I was always the one they missed. Mimi was the only parent who never found out. Other boys' parents hated me. They were always warning their kids not to play with me."

When he was twelve, John enrolled in Quarry Bank High School in the Liverpool suburb of Allerton. The school, now called Calderstones, was named for the nearby limestone quarry that supplied the massive stones for Liverpool Cathedral. Quarry Bank School had a Latin motto, *Ex hoc metalis virtutem,* which means "Out of this rock, you will find truth." Given what rock music meant to him later, John came to find that motto highly symbolic. On his first day he "looked at all the hundreds of new kids and thought, Christ, I'll have to fight all my way through this lot, having just made it at Dovedale."

Within a year, John suffered another personal loss when his Uncle George died suddenly of a brain hemorrhage. The two had become closer over the previous few years as John increasingly turned to George as a refuge from Mimi's stricter ways. Now all John had was another hole in the family.

To compensate, John became the kingpin of another gang of boys at Quarry Bank. "I was aggressive because I wanted to be popular. I wanted to be the leader. It seemed more attractive than just being one of the toffees. I wanted everybody to do what I told them to do: to laugh at my jokes and let me be the boss." The boss became a Teddy boy, what in America in those days was called a juvenile delinquent. He dressed in black with tight pants and sideburns, he drank and smoked, he got into more fights. But he also used his wits, convincing the other boys that he was tough so that he would need to use his fists less and less.

"I was fairly tough at school but I could organize it so it *seemed* like I was tough. I used to dress tough like a Teddy boy, but if I went into the tough districts and came across other Teddy boys I was in danger. A lot of the real Teddy boys were actually in their early twenties. They were dockers, we were only kids. They had hatchets, bicycle chains and real weapons. If somebody like that came in front of us we ran, me and my gang."

At least one of the gang eventually went to prison. And such a future was not out of the question for John Lennon; it certainly must have occured to some of his teachers at school, judging from their reports. "Hopeless," one of them wrote. "He is just wasting other pupils' time." Another teacher proclaimed wrathfully, "Certainly on the road to failure." John's troubles with his teachers eventually escalated to the extent that he got into a fistfight with one of them and was suspended for a week. Officially, he was ranked as the very last student in his class of twenty.

It was 1956. That year the English playwright John Osborne produced his best-known play, *Look Back in*

Anger, which gave rise to the phrase "angry young man." The term referred to Osborne and similar writers of the time whose heroes were rebellious and critical of society, but it was also an apt description of John Lennon. He might very well have been on that road to failure predicted by his teacher.

But then came three interventions: his mother, his headmaster, and music.

By now John's mother, Julia, was living with a man named Robert Dykins, whom John described as "a little waiter with a nervous cough" and who slicked down his hair with margarine. He also had a facial tic, so John called him "Twitchy." Julia and Twitchy had produced two daughters but never got married. And now Julia began to spend more and more time with her son.

They discovered that somehow they'd both developed the same sense of humor and love for words. She did her best to impress John and his pals by acting outrageous— doing things like walking down the street wearing knickers on her head in place of a scarf. And she endeared herself to John by buying him a brightly colored shirt, a new fashion statement that was all the rage in Liverpool but another item on Mimi's list of forbidden pleasures. "Julia became a sort of young aunt to me, or a big sister. As I got bigger and had more rows with Mimi, I used to go and live with Julia for a weekend." John's sense of alienation was somewhat soothed.

Back at Quarry Bank High School there was a new headmaster, Mr. Pobjoy. He knew who the school troublemakers were and on more than one occasion delivered "six of the best" to young Master Lennon. But he also discerned that here was a boy who was "not beyond redemption," largely because of John's ability to draw. Mr. Pobjoy wrote a letter of recommendation to the Liverpool Art College and arranged for an interview. John was accepted for the autumn term of 1957. Julia joined John and Mimi at the house on Menlove Avenue to celebrate.

And then there was music. John's first musical experience, aside from hearing the Salvation Army Band at Strawberry Field, involved the harmonica. When he was eight or nine he bought a cheap one for a bus trip he took to Edinburgh to visit one of Mimi's sisters. He played it all across England and right up to his arrival in the Scottish capital. The bus driver, far from being annoyed, was so impressed by the young man's musicality that he arranged to meet John the next day to give him a high-quality harmonica. That present "really got me going," John remembered. It seems fitting somehow that the Beatles' very first single, "Love Me Do," begins with the sound of John's harmonica.

But John's interest in music would have to wait until that summer of 1956 to fully flower. It was then that the skiffle craze hit England, the first wave of what would soon be the tsunami of rock 'n' roll. Skiffle was very much a people's music, in that a skiffle band included such instruments as a washboard and a tea chest—what in America might be known as a washtub bass—in addition to guitars. The big skiffle hit was a version of the Leadbelly train song "Rock Island Line," sung with a nasal twang by Lonnie Donegan, the Scottish-born musician who died in

November 2002 at the age of seventy-one. The accessible nature of skiffle inspired countless young people to form their own skiffle groups. Guitar sales boomed, the number of instruments sold in England growing from five thousand in 1950 to two hundred fifty thousand in 1957.

In the summer of 1956, a friend told John Lennon about an American rock 'n' roll singer named Elvis Presley, who had recently released a song called "Heartbreak Hotel." At first John was skeptical, thinking the song's name corny and assuming that the singer would sound like Perry Como. But then John heard the song on the radio and knew that the address down on Lonely Street was for him. "Once I heard it and got into it, that was my life, there was no other thing. I thought of nothing else but rock 'n' roll, apart from sex and food and money—but that's all the same thing, really."

John was determined to learn the guitar. Julia, who had learned to play the banjo from Fred Lennon, bought her son a secondhand guitar, "guaranteed not to split," for ten pounds and taught him a few banjo chords. John practiced for hours, first sitting on his bed at Mimi's house and then, when Mimi couldn't stand it anymore and shooed him outside, leaning against the brick wall of the sun porch in front. Mimi told him, "The guitar's all right for a hobby, but you'll never make a living at it." Years later, when John told that story, some Beatles fans in America had those words framed and sent to Mimi; very good-naturedly, she hung them on her wall.

Like many other teenagers in those skiffle-mad days, John decided to form a band. He recruited some friends from Quarry Bank High School and called his group the Quarry Men. John played his guitar, his best friend, Pete Shotton, played the washboard, Rod Davis played the banjo, Colin Hanson played the drums, and a boy named Ivan Vaughan played the tea chest. But Ivan came and went, as did most of the members of the Quarry Men except John and Pete. The band was John's new gang, and of course he had to be the boss. Frequent arguments caused a constant turnover in personnel. So Ivan Vaughan wasn't actually a member of the group on July 6, 1957, when he invited another friend of his, fifteen-year-old Paul McCartney, to come with him to the Woolton Village Fete to hear the Quarry Men perform.

Nineteen fifty-seven was a big year for Paul: that summer he lost his virginity to an older girl who was home baby-sitting for a younger sister while their mother was away. Paul was quite proud of the fact and bragged about his conquest at school the next day. Girls were on his mind a lot that summer, so when Ivan told him that there were likely to be lots of them at the fete, he accepted the invitation eagerly.

According to the program for the fete, the main attractions were stalls, sideshows, ice cream, and lemonade, with tea and other refreshments for sale. At two o'clock that afternoon the festivities commenced with a procession, led by the Band of the Cheshire Yeomanry, that wound through the streets of Woolton and ended in St. Peter's Church Field. At three o'clock the 1957 Rose Queen, Miss Sally Wright, received her crown from the experienced hands of Mrs. Thelwall Jones. Then came a fancy dress parade, with its participants separated into the under-seven-year-old class, the seven- to twelve-year-old class, and the over-twelve-year-old class. At five-fifteen the City of Liverpool police dogs displayed their constabulary talents. And at four-fifteen and again at five-forty-five the crowds were entertained by the Quarry Men Skiffle Group. The Quarry Men were also on the bill for the Grand Dance in the Church Hall at eight o'clock, where they opened for the evening's headliners, the George Edwards Band.

Paul and Ivan arrived at the Church Field while the Quarry Men were on stage. Paul was immediately drawn to the band because they were performing one of his favorite songs, "Come Go with Me," by the Del-Vikings. But he noticed that the young man singing the song, wearing a checked shirt and checking out the crowd beneath his feet, had the words all wrong: instead of "Come little darlin', come and go with me," the leader of the Quarry Men was singing "Down, down, down to the penitentiary" and scat-singing more nonsense words. Paul was intrigued.

Later, in the cool of the evening, Paul and Ivan wandered across the street into the Church Hall, where the Quarry Men were setting up for their eight o'clock gig. Although none of the band members was older than sixteen, there was lots of beer drinking going on. Despite his sexual experience, Paul was not yet a drinker, so to hide his discomfort he sat down at a piano in the corner and began to play some of the songs he'd recently learned: Jerry Lee Lewis's "Whole Lotta Shakin' Goin' On" and a couple of screamers by Little Richard, "Tutti Frutti" and "Long Tall Sally." One by one, the Quarry Men ceased their preparations and turned their attentions to this slightly chubby boy who was wailing away on his own.

Then Paul really captivated them. He borrowed a guitar, tuned it (a procedure that none of them had yet learned), and launched into "Twenty Flight Rock" by Eddie "I went to my congressman and he said, quote, 'I'd like to help you son but you're too young to vote'" Cochran. "Twenty Flight Rock" tells the story of a young man whose girlfriend lives on the twentieth floor of an apartment building with a broken elevator. By the time the guy walks up all those stairs, he laments, "I'm too tired to rock." The song was new and hot in that summer of 1957, and none of the Quarry Men had yet learned all the words or figured out the tricky chords. As Paul was singing, he noticed "this beery old man getting nearer and breathing down my neck. 'What's this old drunk doing?' I thought. Then he said 'Twenty Flight Rock' was one of his favorites. So I knew he was a connoisseur. It was John.

" 'Twenty Flight Rock' . . . that's what got me into the Beatles."

A few days later, Paul was riding his bike through the Allerton golf course when he met Pete Shotton. Pete told Paul that the Quarry Men had been talking about him and would very much like him to join the group. Without much hesitation Paul agreed and gave his first public performance with the band at a dance at Liverpool's Conservative Club. After the dance, Paul played John some songs that he'd written.

John's initial response was unease. He'd had his doubts about inviting Paul to join the Quarry Men because of his feelings of insecurity. "I half thought to myself, 'He's as good as me.' I'd been kingpin up to then. Now, I thought, if I take him on, what will happen? It went through my head that I'd have to keep him in line if I let him join." And now, here was this newcomer writing songs, another threat to John's leadership. But rather than allow his fears to push Paul away, John decided to meet the challenge by writing some songs of his own. He and Paul compared notes, and the two boys soon discovered that they inspired each other in their efforts. They became inseparable, spending long hours at Paul's house on Forthlin Road when they should have been in school, eating fried egg sandwiches and writing songs hour after hour. They also worked on their sound, sometimes standing together in the bathtub to take advantage of the tiled accoustics.

And they talked about their lives at home. John immediately felt close to Paul because of Mary's death, although he couldn't understand Paul's equanimity in the face of his loss. "How can you sit there and act normal with your mother dead?" he demanded. "If anything like that happened to me, I'd go off me head."

In the fall of 1957, John began halfheartedly attending Liverpool Art College. He enjoyed the "arty" atmosphere and the feeling of freedom that came with it, but he didn't care for the classes. He stuck it out because, as he put it, "it was better than working." His real passion was for his music, and he spent hours writing songs with Paul or performing with the Quarry Men. With Paul's arrival, the band changed in John's mind from an occasional avocation to something important. The other Quarry Men soon began to drift off, leaving John and Paul as the irreplaceable core.

Aunt Mimi increasingly voiced her objections to the way John was living his life, and nasty quarrels soon became routine. John found himself spending more time with Julia, to whom he felt profoundly connected. At last they'd come together, after all the disruptions of their earlier years.

And then, one night in the summer of 1958, when John was staying at Julia's house watching TV with Twitchy while Julia was visiting Mimi, an off-duty policeman drove his car into Julia as she crossed Menlove Avenue to catch a bus. She died instantly. The policeman was acquitted of all liability, not that it really mattered. John's mother had abandoned him again.

"It was the worst thing that ever happened to me," John declared years later. "I lost her twice. Once when I was moved in with my auntie. And once again at seventeen when she actually, physically, died. That was very traumatic for me. It made me very, very bitter. The underlying chip on my shoulder that I had got really big then. Being a teenager and a rock 'n' roller and an art student and my mother being killed just when I was re-establishing a relationship with her."

What compels a human being to create has always been a great mystery. But the image of the oyster forming a pearl around a piercing grain of sand provides a clue. Homer in his blindness, Beethoven in his deafness, Bosch in his madness, and countless other artists point to pain as a necessary catalyst. Paul McCartney says that John Lennon never got over his childhood. The loss of their mothers was a deep and lasting bond between them. John said, "All art is pain expressing itself. A lot of people had more pain than me and they've done better things. Genius is pain, too. It's *just* pain."

3

A Flaming Pie

John had told Paul that if anything were to happen to his mother he'd go off his head. For the rest of the summer it seemed to his friends and his fellow students at the art college as if he had done just that. Always a bit caustic and cruel, he became more so. Insults came quickly to his lips. He went out of his way to mock or insult the disabled beggars he encountered on the street. "Where'd your legs go, mate?" he would sneer. "Run away with your wife?" Or "Some people will do anything to get out of the army." He would sneak up behind an elderly gentleman leaning on a cane and shout "Boo!" in his ear. In class at the college he drew sketches of mothers making a loving fuss over babies who were hideously deformed. When Pope Pius XII died on October 9, 1958—John's eighteenth birthday— he drew a disfigured pontiff standing outside the Pearly Gates, rattling them forlornly as they remained closed to him, calling out, "But I'm the Pope, I tell you!"

John also spent hours alone, drinking himself into a fog. Students at the college remember him occasionally sitting

in a stairwell with a bottle between his knees, crying quietly. When he found himself in a crowd of students, more
often than not an argument would break out. A girlfriend
who became the object of John's abuse lashed back at him,
screaming, "Don't take it out on me just because your
mother's dead!"

Fortunately, at this crisis in his life, he could still draw
solace from his music. The Quarry Men, according to
cards they had printed up, promised "Country, Western,
Rock 'n' Roll and Skiffle." The cards said "Open for
engagements," but there had been so much turnover in
personnel that engagements were few. Only John and Paul
were reliable members of the band. But Paul had a pal who
could play a mean guitar. He brought him around for John
to have a listen, and soon thereafter the Quarry Men had a
third guitarist, George Harrison.

George was the youngest Beatle and the only one who
had been spared from heartbreak. His parents, Harold and
Louise, married in 1930 and lived happily in a modest
house in the Wavertree section of Liverpool. Harold, like
Fred Lennon, spent some years as a steward on board
ships, but he eventually settled on dry land as a bus driver.
Louise worked in a grocery until the birth of her first
child, also named Louise, in 1931. Three boys followed:
Harold in 1934, Peter in 1940, and, on February 25,
1943, George.

George had a very warm, very supportive family life. His
mother, Louise, was the sort of mum who always invited the
other kids of the neighborhood in for tea. George attended
Dovedale Primary School, the same school that John

attended, although, since John was three classes ahead, they never met. When George was five, his family moved to a newer house on Upton Green in the Liverpool district of Speke. There was music in the Harrison household, as Harold and Louise directed a beginners' dancing class at a bus drivers' club and they frequently practiced at home. But it wasn't until George was a young teenager starting classes at the Liverpool Institute that he showed any interest in music, thanks in part to a stay in the hospital.

He had been plagued by a series of childhood illnesses before coming down with a case of nephritis, an inflammation of the kidneys. For six weeks he was confined to a bed in Alder Hey Hospital, tired of the spinach he was forced to eat and bored with the inactivity. For reasons he could never quite remember, George decided that when he finally left the hospital he would take up the guitar. A friend of his had a guitar for sale for three pounds and ten shillings; Louise gave George the money and the transaction was made. Harold remembered a chap he'd known at sea who played the guitar and looked him up. The man ran a pub and lived upstairs. Every Thursday night for two or three hours he'd teach young George Harrison the basics of guitar playing, demonstrating new chords and singing him new songs each week.

On school days, George rode the bus to the Liverpool Institute, along a route that included Liverpool's Penny Lane. When he was about thirteen he began to notice another boy on the bus, Paul McCartney. On a trip home from school one day, Paul discovered that he didn't have enough money to pay the fare. George got his mother to pay for Paul, and Mrs. Harrison then characteristically invited Paul in for some tea and biscuits. The two boys learned of their mutual interest in music, and a lifelong friendship was born. Paul and George began to spend hours together after school, and when summer came the two of them spent several weeks hitchhiking through southwest England and Wales.

By this time George's love of the guitar had deepened, and he began to build his own instruments. He acquired a guitar manual and learned more and more chords. Finally he became such a good player that Paul decided to introduce him to his other good friend, John Lennon. At first John doubted that such a youngster—George was two and a half years younger, a big gap at their age—would have anything to offer. But then George launched into the opening guitar riff of "Raunchy," an instrumental hit from 1957 by Bill Justis, a musician from the Sun Records stable run by Sam Phillips. John was so impressed that he asked George to join the Quarry Men on the spot. That song became a running gag in the life of the Beatles; for years afterward, to ease the tedium of touring, John would shout out, "Give us 'Raunchy,' George!"

His "Raunchy" success notwithstanding, it took a while before George felt entirely comfortable around John and his older art college crowd. Total acceptance was a long time coming. But George soon discovered that meekness was not the way to John's heart. "He was very sarcastic, always trying to bring you down, but I either took no notice or gave him the same back," and after a few months the newest member of the Quarry Men felt a measure of welcome. Of George joining the band, John said, "It just worked. Now there were three of us who thought the same."

And now they had two retreats where they could work on their music. Mimi continued to do her best to discourage John from pursuing his rock 'n' roll, and part of her arsenal was a rejection of his new friends. Paul once came pedaling up to the house on Menlove Avenue, knocked on the door, and asked politely, "Hello, Mimi. May I come in?" Her answer: "No, you most certainly may not!" When John first brought George home to meet his aunt, she threw him out because he was wearing a pink shirt. But Louise Harrison welcomed the boys into her home on Upton Green to practice and always made sure they were well fed. No doubt this expression of love and support hastened the arrival of true friendship between John and George.

The McCartney home on Forthlin Road was also a frequent retreat during daylight hours when Jim McCartney was away and the boys should have been at school. Paul recalls that George taught John and him many new chords and that a new chord always occasioned a new song. Slowly at first, the prodigious partnership emerged. John and Paul would sit across from each other with their guitars and play and compose and inspire each other.

"It was great because instead of looking into my own mind for a song," said Paul, "I could see John playing—as if he were holding a mirror to what I was doing." Since neither of them could read or write standard notation, they quickly hit on a formula that not only allowed them to remember their music but also served as a crucial element of quality control: only the songs they could recall from the previous day's work were allowed to survive; they reasoned that if a song didn't make enough of an impression on them to last overnight, how could they expect an audience to remember it?

John frequently came up with a great opening sequence and Paul supplied the bridge. Sometimes the reverse was true. They helped each other with the words. When Paul wrote "I Saw Her Standing There," the original opening line was "Well, she was just seventeen/She'd never been a beauty queen." John didn't like that and suggested the far superior "You know what I mean." Alone at Jim's piano, Paul noodled out a song called "When I'm Sixty-Four." He was still only sixteen. "Love Me Do" was a product of those early sessions, as were many more collaborative efforts. Paul remembers, "I wrote them all down in an exercise book and above them it always said, 'Another Lennon/McCartney Original.'"

Late in 1958, the Quarry Men—at that time John, Paul, George, and two other boys, named Colin Hanton and John "Duff" Lowe—scraped together five pounds among them, showed up at a studio in Liverpool, and made a recording. On one side of the shellac disc they did the Buddy Holly tune "That'll Be the Day" (with John providing the lead vocal), and on the flip side they recorded a Lennon/McCartney original called "In Spite of All the Danger." John and Paul sang, and George took the solo guitar part. Those three, of course, would spend hundreds of hours together in recording studios over the next dozen years, but that primitive recording was the wellspring. It stayed in Duff Lowe's possession until the early 1980s, when he sold it to Paul for what Paul called "a very inflated price."

Over the next year, John, Paul, and George lived the double identities of superheroes: ordinary teenagers by day and Quarry Men by night. John remained at Liverpool Art College, more or less going through the motions. Most of the time he was either with Paul, writing down songs at Forthlin Road, or hanging around Liverpool's Slater Street at a club called the Jacaranda. The Jac, as it was known, was the gathering spot for the city's artists, students, and earnest denizens of what in America was known as the Beat Generation. Strong coffee was served in thick mugs, and aromatic "tea" was smoked by men and women dressed in black, hunched over tiny tables as they discussed art and music, politics, the Bomb, and whether they might spend the coming night together.

Paul was still a student at the Liverpool Institute, half-heartedly preparing for a possible career as a teacher. George, at sixteen, had decided that further schooling was not for him. Jobs were scarce, though, and when he failed an apprenticeship exam, his future looked bleak. A youth employment officer sent him downtown to apply for a job as a window dresser in a big Liverpool department store, but by the time George arrived at the store the position had been filled. Someone at the store offered him a job as an electrician's assistant instead, and over the next several months George learned the rudiments of wiring and laying cables. Most of the time, he admitted later, he spent playing darts.

Nearly every night the three boys played their music, at workingmen's clubs, meeting halls, skating rinks, churches, parties, and the occasional skiffle competition, although skiffle had nearly died out by the last months of 1959. Harold Harrison, thanks to his connection with the Liverpool Bus Company, got them a gig at the Finch Lane Bus Depot, where he and Louise had taught their dance classes. The boys almost never got paid for their efforts, beyond free Cokes and the occasional meal of beans on toast. But they kept at it, honing their harmonies and tightening their sound. Jim McCartney remembered coming home early one day to hear them playing. "I realized then that they were getting good, not just bashing about." And even though there was no obvious reason for believing that their efforts might someday be rewarded, the three boys maintained a consistent level of optimism. "We all had an amazing, positive feeling about being in the band full-time," said George. "I don't know why—we were just cocky. Something good was going to happen."

They managed to infuse their music-making with that same youthful optimism and enthusiasm, which in turn helped to fuel those very feelings of hope. From the first, then, the band reflected itself in its music, much as John was a mirror to Paul when they wrote their songs.

In August 1959, John, Paul, and George helped open a new venue in Liverpool, one that would prove to be an important way station in the early years of their career: the

Casbah Coffee Club. The Casbah was the creation of Mona Best, the daughter of an Irish major in the English army who was stationed in India. Mona was born in India, where she met a captain named John Best, the British army middleweight boxing champion, and moved with him to his hometown of Liverpool in 1945. In 1957, with sons Rory and Pete, the Bests moved into a rambling house at 8 Haymans Green in the Liverpool suburb of West Derby. Two years later, after watching a TV program about coffee bars in London's Soho district, Mona Best declared that she wanted to build a coffee bar in the basement. It would, she announced, be called the Casbah, after a line uttered by actor Charles Boyer in one of her favorite movies, *Algiers*. Those words, she hoped, would soon be on the lips of every young music lover in Liverpool: "Come with me to the Casbah!"

Throughout the summer of 1959, the Best family and many young recruits helped turn the basement into a club. Mona chose August 29 as opening night, and through the grapevine of the burgeoning Liverpool music scene, she hired the Quarry Men as her opening act. John, Paul, and George pitched in with the preparations. John painted his impressions of African art on the ceiling of the dance room, Paul painted a rainbow on the ceiling over the stage, and George added some stars above the coffee bar. On Saturday night the 29th, the band took the stage, and John shouted out, "Hi everyone, welcome to the Casbah. We're the Quarry Men and we're gonna play you some rock 'n' roll!" It would prove to be the first of many appearances by the band at Haymans Green.

By this time, the name Quarry Men was on its way out. Only John, Paul, and George were permanent members of the band now. They had no regular drummer, and the boys who occasionally sat in had none of the other three's commitment. At one of their gigs, pianist Duff Lowe looked at his watch in the middle of a set, realized that he'd promised his father that he'd be home soon, and abruptly walked off the stand, leaving the rest of the band to finish the set as best they could. As none of the boys attended Quarry Bank High School anymore, it seemed foolish to retain the name, and the band began to perform under a series of names, some of them lasting only a few days. For one gig they all showed up wearing different colored shirts, so for that night they performed as the Rainbows. For a talent show in Manchester put on by a television personality named Carroll Levis, who called himself "Mr. Star-Maker," John, Paul, and George performed as Johnny and the Moondogs. Mr. Star-Maker's shtick was a device that registered how much applause each act received at the end of the evening. John had played his "guaranteed not to crack" guitar so much and so furiously that it had indeed split wide open, so for the culmination of the contest he stood between Paul and George, one hand on each of their shoulders as they played their intact guitars, singing Buddy Holly's "Think It Over." The boys thought that they had performed quite well, but, as they had to catch the last train home to Liverpool before the show's end, they never had the chance to move the needle and learn how much Manchester loved the Moondogs.

It was the end of 1959, the end of the decade that witnessed the birth of rock 'n' roll. As the 1960s—the decade
synonymous with the Beatles—began, John, Paul, and
George welcomed a new member into their band, someone whose influence on them, and by extension on us,
vastly exceeded his minimal musical ability: Stuart Sutcliffe.

Stu was a Scotsman, born in Edinburgh (the glorious
capital city where John acquired his good harmonica)
on June 23, 1940. By the late 1950s he was living in
Liverpool, attending the art college, when he met John at
the Jacaranda. Unlike John, Stuart was a serious student
and had a considerable and widely acknowledged talent.
He was also extremely attractive, in a dark, moody, James
Dean-ish way, and he was known for his monkish, gen-
uinely artistic mode of living. His tiny flat on Gambier
Terrace could have been used as a set for Rodolfo's garret
in *La Boheme;* in fact, in a scene straight out of Puccini's
opera, Stu had to sacrifice a set of chairs to the fireplace to
keep warm during the winter. When they met, in the bleak
aftermath of Julia's death, Stu and John took to each other
immediately. Stu wasn't put off by John's grief and in fact
was drawn to the musician's charisma and energy. John
found Stu intellectually and spiritually stimulating and
admired his knowledge and passion for the arts. The two
would often go off together for hours, discussing trends in
art and design, and for a time John moved in with Stu,
making the cramped flat feel even smaller but much more
convivial.

Stu began to attend some of John's gigs and also to
raise the ire of John's band mates. Paul later admitted to

feelings of jealousy for Stu, as he obviously had captured a part of John unknown to his fellow musicians. George may have shared some of Paul's feelings, but as the youngest of the trio, he appreciated Stu for never making him feel inferior because he didn't attend the art college. Stu made it plain that he admired the whole band tremendously and even arranged a few gigs for them to play, which took some of the edge off the rivalry. John saw Stu's interest in the band as a validation of their confidence in themselves. "He was always saying how good we were when nobody else was very impressed."

Stu also helped in more practical ways. With Stu's lobbying assistance, John managed to convince the authorities at the art college to purchase a tape recorder and a public address system. The two students pointed out the equipment's benefit to the school, but once the gear arrived John appropriated it for his own use.

In December 1959, Stuart Sutcliffe achieved some notoriety of his own. A wealthy Liverpool art collector named John Moore bought one of Stu's paintings for sixty-five pounds (nearly one hundred fifty dollars), a most tidy sum for an impoverished artist. Expecting to use the money for paints or canvases, or at least the rent or some new chairs for his flat, Stu instead found himself the object of some intense wheedling from John and Paul over a cappuccino at the Casbah Club. Stu had expressed such admiration for the band, John said, that the obvious thing to do with the money was to buy a bass guitar and join them. Stu eventually gave in and spent the entire sixty-five pounds on an enormous Hofner bass. A rather slight man, Stu was nearly dwarfed by the big instrument. He couldn't play it, either, but his new friends promised they would teach him the basics. By Christmas, Stu had joined the band.

Within a very few months Stu helped the band to discover its name. One night at Stu's flat in April 1960, John admitted that he was envious of Buddy Holly's band, the Crickets. It would be a wonderful name for an English band, John said, because of the double meaning, referring both to the insect and the English game of cricket. Too bad it was already taken. Well, how about another insect, suggested Stu; how about beetles? It occurred to John that by spelling the word with an "a" they could create the double meaning of insect and beat music. The next evening, Paul recalls, while walking near Liverpool Cathedral, John and Stuart announced to Paul and George that they wanted to call the band the Beatles.

A few years later, John gave a fanciful explanation of the origin of the name in a typical bit of wordplay that he said had been "translated from the John Lennon." "Many people ask what are Beatles? How did the name arrive? So we will tell you. It came in a vision—a man appeared on a flaming pie and said unto them, 'From this day on you are Beatles with an A.' 'Thank you, Mister Man,' they said, thanking him." In 1997, Paul McCartney paid tribute to John's "vision" by naming one of his albums *Flaming Pie*.

In May 1960, the Beatles went on the road for the first time, and the road led north. That year a well-known promoter from London, Larry Parnes, came to Liverpool in search of new talent. He had already signed up a number of singers, always giving them aggressive names such as Billy Fury and Marty Wilde.

Allan Williams, the Welsh-born owner of the Jacaranda Club, arranged an audition for a number of Liverpool bands, including the Beatles. As they still didn't have a permanent drummer, they secured the services of Johnny Hutchinson, who played drums with a band called Cass and the Casanovas. Cass, whose real name was Brian Casser, let John Lennon know that he thought the name Beatles was a terrible choice. They should emulate him and spotlight their leader. With a piratical turn of phrase, Cass suggested that John should become Long John Silver, or at the very least his group should be known as Long John and the Silver Beatles. John accepted part of this advice from a more experienced musician, and his band played the Parnes audition as the Silver Beatles. To their delight, Parnes offered them a two-week tour of Scotland backing up another of his young stars, Johnny Gentle.

To get permission for the trip, Paul told his father that the Liverpool Institute had suddenly announced a two-week holiday. George quit his electrician job, and John and Stuart simply disappeared from the art college for a fortnight. They hired a drummer named Tommy Moore, a forklift operator at the Garston Bottle Works, and set off for Scotland. To anyone else, the tour would have seemed a disaster; it was a succession of one-night stands playing for tiny crowds in tiny towns. They ate poorly and slept in cold-water hotels. John and Tommy Moore decided they couldn't stand each other, and the drummer quit the moment they returned to Liverpool. But they had been paid thirty-six pounds for their two weeks' work, and the name Silver Beatles had appeared on posters. They were professionals. They had begun.

Unfortunately, back in Liverpool they struggled. They played a few dates at the Casbah for three pounds a night. With Paul playing the drums, they accompanied exotic dancers named Janice and Shirley at the New Cabaret Artists Club, a strip joint run by the same Allan Williams who owned the Jacaranda and had gotten them the audition with Larry Parnes. And they played a succession of dates at dance halls and dives in neighborhoods that were dangerous after dark, Bootle and Garston and Wallasey and Litherland. The Teddy boys and their girls—called Judies—who showed up for these shows were less interested in the music than in starting fights and spilling a little blood along with their beer. The fights were usually confined to the back of the halls, but one night in Litherland the Silver Beatles were ambushed by a gang of Teds in the parking lot after the show. Stu Sutcliffe was thrown to the ground and kicked in the head a number of times before John managed to drag him off. It took days for Stu to recover from the beating, if he ever really did.

The Silver Beatles were one of many groups in Liverpool at the time, vying for public attention with such bands as Rory Storm and the Hurricanes, Cass and the Casanovas, Gerry and the Pacemakers, Derry and the Seniors, Faron's Flamingos, Lee Curtis and the All Stars, and the Swinging Blue Jeans. As talented as the Silver Beatles were, they might never have emerged from the Mersey sound with their own distinctive voice had not lightning struck in the form of another tour. As it happened, the tour was not so much lightning as *blitz:* their destination was Hamburg, Germany. "I grew up in Hamburg, not Liverpool," said John Lennon. The same could be said of the Beatles.

4

Laboratory and Conservatory

In the summer of 1960, the city of Hamburg had been a prominent destination for nearly eight hundred years. Though it lies sixty-five miles from the North Sea, Hamburg is connected to the sea and the wider world beyond by the broad waters of the river Elbe. The emperor Barbarossa issued a decree in the twelfth century granting the inhabitants of Hamburg the privilege of duty-free shipping along the Elbe, and ever since the city has enjoyed its status as the most important German port. Trade and commerce have been close to Hamburg's heart for centuries; its stock exchange, Germany's first, dates from 1558, and its flourishing fish market has been a staple of dockside life since 1703. But music has also sounded through the streets of Hamburg throughout its long history. The great composers Felix Mendelssohn and Johannes Brahms were born there in the nineteenth century, and for more than forty years in the mid-eighteenth century, the city's court orchestra was led by Georg Philip Telemann.

Violence and rowdyism have long been staples of life along the Elbe waterfront. Dockside brawls were common when ships from around the globe tied up and sailors speaking every conceivable tongue staggered down the gangways. The city's musicians were by no means sheltered from the storm; Brahms witnessed his share of fistfights when he played the piano in pierside whorehouses, and the composers Georg Friedrich Handel and Johann Mattheson fought a near-fatal duel in a Hamburg opera house after quarreling about conducting.

With seagoing commerce and music-making such important aspects of its personality, Hamburg is very much a German version of Liverpool. The two cities have similar weather—"damp and cold most days of the year, just like most of the people," as a German wit observed—and both can be found on a map at roughly 53 degrees north latitude. Both cities suffered great damage from the air during World War II. Fifty-five thousand people were killed when the RAF firebombed Hamburg in 1943 and 1944.

Perhaps it was just a cosmic coincidence that brought the Beatles to Hamburg, but there's no question that their time in Germany was crucial to their development as artists. When they arrived in 1960 they and their music were raw and undisciplined, and when they returned to England from their last visit to Hamburg two years later they were a tight and popular band on the brink of stardom.

Allan Williams, who by this time was sporting cards

announcing that he enjoyed "sole direction" of the Beatles, made the German connection possible. His contact was a former magician and circus clown turned sharp-eyed businessman named Bruno Koschmider. At a club in London, Williams convinced Koschmider that he needed a British beat group to pull customers into his clubs in Hamburg, and the Englishman suggested Derry and the Seniors. Some weeks later Koschmider wrote to Williams, telling him that the Seniors were a success and asking for another Liverpool band to perform at another one of his clubs. Williams proposed the Silver Beatles, and the deal was done. The band would be paid fifteen pounds a week for a two-month engagement.

But Koschmider wanted another five-piece band, like Derry and the Seniors, and the Silver Beatles had only four permanent members: John, Paul, George, and Stu. They would have to find a fifth in a hurry. Fortunately, the solution to this problem could solve another: the group's lack of a reliable drummer. George recommended Pete Best, the eighteen-year-old son of Mona Best, the proprietor of the Casbah Club. Pete had gotten a new drum kit for Christmas and had started playing at the Casbah with a group called the Blackjacks. Paul called Pete, told him about the Hamburg gig, and asked him to audition. The next day, at another Allan Williams club, the Blue Angel, Pete Best played a half-dozen numbers in the course of fifteen minutes. Afterward, John, Paul, George, and Stu conferred in a private room at the club before coming out and telling Pete, "You're in!" Williams confessed later that the audition was a sham; the boys were desperate for a drummer but didn't want to let Pete know for fear that he'd ask for more money. So with that bit of subterfuge behind them, the Beatles were ready for Germany. And now they were five.

On August 16, 1960, the day they left Britain for the first time, the boys piled into a green-and-cream-colored van driven by Allan Williams. The band's equipment and suitcases, which contained new custom-made lilac jackets stitched together by a tailor Paul knew, were strapped to the top. George, not quite six months past his seventeenth birthday, was clutching a tin of homemade scones his mother had baked him. Williams drove the boys from Liverpool via London to Harwich, where the van was hoisted onto a ferry for the trip across the English Channel. During the crossing, Williams informed the boys that they were technically entering the continent illegally, as he hadn't managed to acquire work permits for them. If anyone raised the question, he told them quietly, they should claim to be students. In a demonstration of just how concerned he was over Williams's dishonesty, John shoplifted a new harmonica when they landed in Holland.

The Hamburg district where they lived and worked, St. Pauli, was then and remains today a collection of dim bars, garish souvenir stores, sex shops, and houses of the illest repute. Just steps from the Elbe River docks, St. Pauli afforded incoming sailors and local dock workers a cornucopia of the world's most enticing vices. Drug dealing, gunrunning, high-stakes gambling, street fights, day- and nightlong drinking binges, and every sexual practice under the sun and moon were so common in St. Pauli as to be utterly unremarkable to the district's clientele. The reddest lights were along the Reeperbahn, the notorious main street. Just off the Reeperbahn was a shorter but no less mean street called the Grosse Freiheit. It was here that Allan Williams opened the doors of his van and the five boys emerged.

"The Liverpool scene was much more innocent and teenage," remembered Paul. "The Reeperbahn was hookers and strip clubs. It was great for us—we didn't have any complaints at all. It was like we were sailors and this was our first voyage, a voyage to Hamburg."

On the voyage from Liverpool, the band members had decided to drop the "Silver" from their name. When Bruno Koschmider escorted them to their digs, John spotted a poster advertising the Silver Beatles and promptly crossed out the offending adjective with a black pen. But the poster turned out to be the least of their worries. The Beatles learned that they were booked to play at a dead-end club called the Indra instead of at Koschmider's Kaiserkeller, where Derry and the Seniors were holding forth. Outside, the Indra's most appealing feature was a neon sign in the shape of an elephant. Inside, the club was tiny, dirty, and smelly, and offered an assortment of strippers and sex shows to a crowd of gangsters, drug dealers, and transvestites. On the bright side, there usually weren't more than half a dozen people in the club at any one time. That little attendance problem was what Bruno Koschmider had brought the Beatles to Hamburg to fix.

But he certainly had no plans to coddle them. He put them up at a nearby cinema, the Bambi Kino, which featured a never-ending series of porn films. Their rooms, bare concrete affairs with thin cots and no windows, were right behind the screen, and after a long night of playing they would often be awakened by the groans and grunts of the early show. They were allowed to wash in the men's toilets of the cinema. The whole arrangement, said Pete Best, "was like the Black Hole of Calcutta."

Back at the Indra, their dressing room was also the men's room. But again there was a bright side to that situation: they had very little time to spend there. Koschmider told them that they were expected to perform eight or nine hours a night, often seven nights a week, starting at seven o'clock in the evening and running until two or three in the morning. On Saturday nights, their call was 6 P.M. It was a killer schedule, but in the long run it gave new life to the band.

On their Scottish tour with Johnny Gentle, the Beatles had never played for more than twenty minutes at a time; Johnny was the headliner, after all. Back home in Liverpool, the Beatles' gigs had usually lasted forty-five minutes or an hour, so they quickly learned which of their songs were the most popular and played the same ones every night. But in Hamburg they had to fill much more time, so they were forced to learn new material and to expand on what they already knew.

"We had to learn millions of songs," said George. "We'd get a Chuck Berry record and learn it all. Same with Little Richard, the Everly Brothers, Buddy Holly, Fats Domino, Gene Vincent, everything." And their tried-and-true numbers evolved, as they discovered the secrets of improvisation and the art of listening to each other. "Each song lasted twenty minutes and had twenty solos in it," said John. "That's what improved the playing."

On stage they'd often exchange insults with their mostly drunk audience. "We used to shout in English at the Germans," recalled John. "Call them Nazis and tell them to fuck off." It was all according to plan, or at least their interpretation of the directions given them on their second night by Bruno Koschmider. Though he knew nothing about music, Koschmider's circus background led him to believe that he knew a thing or two about show business. The important thing, he told his young charges, was to make a show for the customers; that is, make a big noise and big gestures. He would stand at the back of the Indra, calling out, *"Mach shau! Mach schau!"* So the Beatles would make the biggest show they could, leaping and prancing around the tiny stage, John doing his best impression of cripples and spastics, Paul repeating the chorus of the Ray Charles hit "What'd I Say?" for more than thirty minutes.

Staying awake and keeping fed were definite challenges under the circumstances. The band often ate onstage, grabbing a bite of nourishment on the fly. From a washroom attendant named Rosa, the boys learned of the stimulating effects of little diet pills called Preludin, which she stored in a candy jar; grabbing and downing a handful of "Prellys" made it possible to keep to the schedule. Other stimulants also came within easy reach. "We had lots of girls," said Pete Best. "We soon realized they were easy to get. Everything improved one hundred percent. We'd been meek and mild musicians at first, now we became a powerhouse." Along with the power, however, they acquired the usual assortment of venereal diseases. Luckily, they found themselves within walking distance of the reliable German public health facilities.

Playing incredibly long hours under very difficult conditions while living in such squalor might well have convinced the boys that it all wasn't worth it . . . except that, miles away from home and speaking a foreign language, they really had nowhere else to go and had to depend on themselves. "We got better and got more confidence," said John. "We couldn't help it, with all the experience, playing all night long. It was handy, them being foreign. We had to try even harder, put our heart and soul into it, to put ourselves over."

"Hamburg was really like our apprenticeship," said George, "learning how to play in front of people." Stu Sutcliffe wrote home to his parents, "We have improved a thousand-fold since our arrival and Allan Williams, who is here at the moment, tells us that there is no band in Liverpool to touch us."

Slowly, the word began to spread up and down the Reeperbahn that these crazy Englishmen were making a very good show. Attendance soared. But so many people began packing into the Indra that neighbors and local church officials began to complain about the noise. Before the Beatles' two-month booking was up, police shut the Indra down. Bruno Koschmider merely shrugged and moved the Beatles to the venue they'd hoped to occupy from the beginning, the Kaiserkeller.

Derry and the Seniors by now had gone home. Rather than settle for a single English attraction, Koschmider requested that Allan Williams send another band for him to book. So within days of taking up residence in the Kaiserkeller, the Beatles found themselves sharing the bill with what was probably the top Liverpool band at the time, Rory Storm and the Hurricanes. Rory's real name was Alan Caldwell. He was tall and dashing and usually appeared onstage in a flashy gold suit. His lead guitar player, born John Byrne, had renamed himself Johnny Guitar. His drummer, a Liverpool lad named Richard Starkey, was known as Ringo Starr.

Richard Starkey Junior, to be absolutely accurate, was born on July 7, 1940, three months before John Lennon, to Elsie Gleave and Richard Starkey Senior. His parents both worked at the same bakery, and little Ritchie, as he was called, always could count on a plentiful supply of sugar in the house. But there was little else that was sweet about Ritchie's childhood. Although much was later made of the Beatles' working-class backgrounds, it was really only Ritchie who came from the wrong side of Liverpool's tracks. The Starkeys lived in the Dingle, a rough area of tenement housing near the Pier Head. Richard Senior walked out on his family in 1943, leaving Elsie to find work as a barmaid to keep her child in sugar. Her job required her to be away from home much of the day, and Ritchie often stared mournfully out the window, observing to his mother as she walked out the door, "I wish I had brothers and sisters. There's nobody to talk to when it's raining."

Ritchie's health was poor. He started school at St. Silas when he was five, but within a year his appendix burst, he developed peritonitis, and he sank into a coma that lasted for ten weeks. Three times doctors told Elsie that Ritchie would be dead by the next morning. His recovery took a full year, by which time he had missed so much school that he could neither read nor write. Back in St. Silas, he was stuck in a class and largely ignored by his teachers. A few times he tried to skip school by producing notes supposedly written by his mother. But the notes were always so badly spelled that the authorities easily figured out their author's identity. When Ritchie was nine years old, a neighbor named Marie Maguire, the daughter of one of Elsie's longtime friends, taught him the rudiments of literacy, and he rewarded her with a bottle of perfume from Woolworth's.

Elsie married a housepainter named Harry Graves, and Ritchie took to him well. "He was a really sweet guy; all animals and children loved him," says Ringo today. "I learned gentleness from Harry." Harry bought the boy DC comics and played him Sarah Vaughan records. But Ritchie's health betrayed him again. At thirteen he developed a bad cold that turned into pleurisy and landed him back in the hospital for another two years. He learned knitting while lying in bed, but he never returned to school. Harry found him a job as a messenger boy for British Railways and then a position as an apprentice joiner at a local engineering firm. At least, thought Ritchie, he'd have a trade.

But then he, too, was swept away by the skiffle craze. Harry bought him a drum set for ten pounds, and he helped form a band called the Eddie Clayton Skiffle Group. By the time skiffle died, Ritchie had become an accomplished drummer. He and a friend thought of emigrating to Houston, Texas, because their musical hero, Lightnin' Hopkins, came from there. They went so far as to go to the U.S. consulate and acquire the necessary forms. But when they found out that they had to answer "questions like 'Was your mother's grandmother's Great Dane a communist?'" they decided to stay put. By 1959 Ritchie was drumming professionally with Rory Storm. Also by then Rory had suggested that because he sported so many rings, he should change his name to Ringo Starr. By the autumn of 1960, when the Hurricanes hit Hamburg, Ringo was indeed a minor star.

He certainly seemed a star to the Beatles. He was older than all of them except for Stuart, he sported a beard, and, most impressive of all, he had his own car. And as a musician Ringo could boast of gigs at Butlin's Holiday Camp, a venue that paid extremely well. So when Rory Storm and the Hurricanes blew into the Kaiserkeller, the Beatles felt fortunate to share the stage.

Bruno Koschmider decided to take advantage of having both bands on the bill at the same time. He had each band play for an hour, then take an hour off while the other band performed. This meant that Kaiserkeller customers could enjoy twelve straight hours of rock 'n' roll while the musicians, who played for only six hours but couldn't afford to leave the club for fear of missing their next set, were essentially employed for twelve-hour shifts. During the hours when the Hurricanes weren't playing, Ringo often sat out front and listened to the Beatles perform, occasionally calling out requests. There would be times away from the club when Pete Best would go off by himself and Ringo would join the rest of the Beatles for a drink; slowly, a working friendship began to grow, one that would reach its full bloom two years later.

Soon another important friendship emerged. One night a Hamburg art student named Klaus Voorman had an argument with his girlfriend. Steamed about the dispute, Voorman was wandering down the Reeperbahn in search of diversion when he heard some loud music coming from a basement on the Grosse Freiheit. He walked down the steps of the Kaiserkeller, where Rory Storm was just finishing a set. He stayed to hear the Beatles, then the Hurricanes again, and then, once more, the Beatles. Thrilled by the music and forgetting all about his earlier argument, Voorman rushed home to tell his girlfriend what he'd seen and heard. Within days she joined him at the Kaiserkeller. Her name was Astrid Kirchherr.

The Beatles were great artists who worked hard to develop their gifts. They were also very lucky in their acquaintances, and one of the most significant of them was Astrid. She was a lovely young woman, twenty-two years old, with a gamine face and figure, a distinctive pixie haircut, and an unerring sense of fashion. She was a photographer with a keen eye for shadings and settings. She brought the Beatles to a deserted fairground near Hamburg and took some stunning photographs that revealed to her camera and to her subjects the sensitive depths of their personalities. She looked so good in her black leather outfits that she soon had them dressing in leather as well. And, one by one, she convinced them to cut their hair in bangs and brush it well over their foreheads in an approximation of her own hairstyle. Thus was born the Beatle haircut. "Astrid was the one, really, who influenced our image more than anybody," said George. "She made us look great."

Astrid fell deeply in love with Stu Sutcliffe and he with her. Within a few weeks she ended her relationship with Klaus Voorman and became engaged to Stu. They purchased rings together, and Stu told his bandmates that once they were married he intended to stay in Germany to live with her. For the young Scotsman, who'd always felt more than a bit slighted by the Liverpudlians, Astrid's attentions were a welcome change. Stu wrote home to friends that Astrid "thought that I was the most handsome of the lot. Here was I, feeling the most insipid working member of the group, being told how much superior I looked—this alongside the great Romeo John Lennon and his two stalwarts Paul and George, the Casanovas of Hamburg!"

For all any of the great lovers knew then, they might just remain in Germany with Stu and Astrid and never return to England. They were packing in customers at the Kaiserkeller and were starting to entertain offers from other venues as well. One of the English rock singers they most admired, Tony Sheridan, was performing regularly at a higher-class Hamburg establishment called the Top Ten Club. The owner of the Top Ten, Peter Eckhorn, made the Beatles a very attractive offer to come to his club; he would pay them more money and provide very comfortable living quarters upstairs. It was an offer too good to refuse, but word of the pending deal reached the ears of Bruno Koschmider. Rather than lose the Beatles to a rival club, he engineered their expulsion from Germany.

Although Allan Williams had warned them on the journey to Germany that he had failed to secure work permits for them, the issue hadn't arisen during the three months they had been in Hamburg. But then, just as they were about to accept the offer from Eckhorn, it did, with a vengeance. As they were moving their gear into their new digs above the Top Ten, policemen marched in and demanded to see their papers. Since George was still only seventeen years old and the Reeperbahn curfews prohibited anyone under eighteen from being out after ten o'clock, he was ruled to have consistently, and with malice aforethought, broken the law. The police informed him that he had twenty-four hours to pack up his things and leave the country.

That night, November 21, Astrid and Stu drove George to the train station for his journey home to Liverpool. Within days, Paul and Pete followed him. They made a final visit to the Bambi Kino to collect what was left of their belongings, and, as a sort of puerile parting shot at Koschmider, they hung a condom on the wall and set fire to it. Again the *polizei* tracked them down and this time hauled them into the station on arson charges. After a tense two or three hours, they, too, were ordered to leave Germany at once. With no band to play with, John also left for Liverpool. Stu remained in the arms of Astrid for a few more weeks until an attack of tonsillitis convinced them both that he should seek care at home. Astrid bought Stu a plane ticket and he, alone among the Beatles, traveled back to Liverpool in high style.

"The Hamburg Retreat, I always call it," remembers Pete Best. "We went out there as five but came back in dribs and drabs." Paul jokes, "We went as kids and came back as . . . old kids!" But what they didn't know, at least at first, was just how good a band they had become by the time they came home from Hamburg.

It took them several weeks to realize it. It was early December 1960. George, unaware that his mates had followed so soon, thought he was alone in Liverpool. John, with no desire to return to art college and depressed to be back with Mimi in the house on Menlove Avenue, spent days lying in bed. Paul, at the urging of his father, took a job delivering Christmas packages for a firm called Speedy Prompt Delivery, or SPD, for seven pounds a week. Stu was still in Hamburg with Astrid. For the moment, the Beatles were moribund.

But Pete Best persuaded his mother, Mona, to book the band at the Casbah. He and his friend Neil Aspinall, who at the time was rooming at the house on Haymans Green, started putting up posters around Liverpool announcing "The Beatles Are Coming." Mona billed their appearance as "The Return of the Fabulous Beatles, Direct from Hamburg" and set the date for December 17. With Stu still abroad, Pete asked his former Blackjacks bassist, Chas Newby, to fill in.

That night, as Pete recalls, was a revelation to everyone. Paul kicked things off with Little Richard's "Long Tall Sally," just as he had sung it in Hamburg, "and you could physically feel the crowd gasp. When we finished the first number the place went into rapture, it just exploded. We took the roof off the place. That was the Beatles' sound, it was big, it was raw, it was savage. We didn't realise we were doing anything different, but it was the start of the onslaught."

Two days after Christmas they made a return visit to the Litherland Town Hall, where the band had been mugged and Stuart so badly beaten. This time there was no trouble. And the reception was as rapturous as the one at the Casbah had been; more so, as the Litherland Town Hall held a much larger crowd. Nobody, including the Beatles themselves at first, could figure out what had happened on the Continent, but their musical immersion on the banks of the Elbe had quite clearly, and profoundly, transformed them.

Hamburg had been both their laboratory and their conservatory, the site of the sort of forced experimentation, discovery, and thorough musical education that would never have befallen them had they stayed in Liverpool. They had found their sound, and they had discovered their voice. It is a signal moment in the life of any artist, the way a writer needs to find a voice, a painter a vision, an actor a fully formed character after he puts aside the script. During those long nights along the Reeperbahn the Beatles, perhaps unconsciously, had read from the rhythmic scripts of Buddy Holly and Fats Domino, of Gene Vincent and Little Richard, and had absorbed all they needed to learn from the styles and licks of their teachers. Before he is ready to soar on his own, a budding composer needs to write out countless fugues and learn in his bones the rules about parallel fifths. And then he needs to find his voice.

"It was Hamburg that had done it," declared John. "That's where we'd really developed. To keep it up for twelve hours at a time, we'd really had to hammer. We would never have developed as much if we'd stayed at home. We had to try anything that came into our heads in Hamburg. There was nobody to copy from."

In speaking those words, John Lennon was echoing what another great composer once said about his immersion in isolation. The Austrian master Franz Joseph Haydn spent years as a young man serving as court musician to the Esterhazy family at their remote castle on the plains of central Hungary, miles from the musical capitals of Vienna or Prague. Years later, now the most famous musician in Europe, Haydn looked back on his Esterhazy days and wrote, "I was cut off from the world. There was no one near to confuse or torment me, so I was forced to become original."

Those few, those happy few, listeners who had heard the Beatles before their trip to Germany were in a position to appreciate fully the metamorphosis that had occured. There would be so many more, of course; that's a large measure of what we, those of us who came along later, loved about them as the Sixties deepened, how they always changed and grew and bloomed brighter and more vivid to our eyes and to our ears. But the first big change came before we met the Beatles in 1964. Hamburg was where it happened. To paraphrase the motto of Quarry Bank High School, Hamburg was the rock out of which the Beatles found their truth.

5

The Toppermost of the Poppermost

As 1961 dawned, so, too, did Beatlemania.

"Suddenly," said John Lennon, "we were a wow." Pete Best and his mother, Mona, found booking the band to be an easy job, as more venues in and around Liverpool began clamoring for their services. For some weeks, many fans expressed their amazement that the boys spoke English as well as they did; thanks to Mona's posters billing the Beatles as "direct from Hamburg," many in the crowds assumed the band was German. As Mona's advertising also referred to "The Fabulous Beatles Rock Combo," it became increasingly common to refer to them as The Fabs, the derivation of the later, and ubiquitous, nickname "the Fab Four."

Mona Best was instrumental in finding the Beatles their best-known permanent gig, the Cavern Club. The basement of a former fruit and vegetable warehouse, centrally located at 10 Mathew Street in Liverpool, the Cavern had

61

maintained a somewhat snooty jazz-only policy for years. Mona called up the Cavern's owner, Ray McFall, and, telling him of the Beatles' successful run at the Casbah, helped convince him that a "rock combo" would bring in far more customers for him. At a lunchtime concert on February 9, the Beatles made the first of what would turn out to be hundreds of appearances at the Cavern over the next two and a half years.

True to its name, the Cavern was dark, dank, and fairly foul. There was no ventilation, and the walls usually were covered with a slick and sweaty condensation. It was also a small space, with three vaulted archways providing just enough headroom for the performers to move about gingerly on the tiny stage. But the intimacy helped forge a bond between the band and its mostly young audience. Many of them came to dance but stayed to listen, as the Beatles captivated them with a sound and style that demanded close attention. Rapidly, though, attentiveness gave way to adoration, and pandemonium became a regular part of the proceedings. On Valentine's Day, Paul sang the German song "Wooden Heart," which he'd begun to perform in Hamburg, wearing a red satin heart inscribed with the Beatles' names pinned to his jacket. After the concert the heart was raffled off as a door prize, and when the winner came forward to claim her heart and a kiss from Paul, a crush of shrieking girls rushed the stage, and the band had to be escorted to safety by the Cavern's beefy bouncers.

Over the next six weeks, the Beatles generally performed six days a week, sometimes at two or three different venues a day. They continued their regular appearances at the Casbah Club and the Cavern and also played at ballrooms, town halls, social clubs, and such locales as the Aintree Institute and the Liverpool Jazz Society. They occasionally shared the bill with other Liverpool bands, such as Rory Storm and the Hurricanes, Gerry and the Pacemakers, the Swinging Blue Jeans, and Kingsize Taylor and the Dominoes. But it slowly began to dawn on the Beatles that they were the center of attention. "It took us a while to realize how much better we'd become than the other groups," said George. "When we did, and saw that we were getting the big crowds everywhere, we realized that part of the reason was that for the first time people were following us around, coming to see us personally, not just coming to dance."

Now that the Beatles were on the go a lot, they decided that they needed someone to help with the travel and assist with the gear. They chose Neil Aspinall, who had known Paul, George, and John since their school days and who had been living in Pete Best's house in West Derby, to be their road manager. At the time, Neil was studying to be an accountant, but he chucked it all for a life of driving vans and fetching and carrying for the band. Within a very short time, Neil realized that his decision represented a huge entry on the plus side of his life's ledger.

Meanwhile, Peter Eckhorn, the manager of Hamburg's Top Ten Club, was still intent on showcasing the wild young Englishmen. There remained the uncomfortable fact of their ignominious exit from Germany the previous autumn, but George had turned eighteen years old in

February and was now of legal age. And between them, Peter Eckhorn and Allan Williams—who still saw himself as the Beatles' representative—wrote enough letters to the right authorities to secure fully valid visas and work permits. The band left Liverpool by train on March 27 and on April 1 began a three-month stint at the Top Ten, located at 136 Reeperbahn, around the corner from the Grosse Freiheit and the Kaiserkeller. They were set to earn thirty-five deutschmarks per man per day, almost twice what Bruno Koschmider had paid them, but their terms of employment were still quite taxing. They were expected to perform for seven hours each evening, Monday through Friday, and for eight hours on weekends, with a scant fifteen-minute break every hour. Their accommodations were an improvement over the Bambi Kino but were still rather spartan. They slept in five bunk beds in an apartment on the fourth floor above the Top Ten, their ablutions overseen by a heavyset washroom attendant known as Mutti, or Mommy.

The Beatles were headliners at the Top Ten, but they also backed up other acts, including the English singer Tony Sheridan. Sheridan had had quite a following for a time, appearing on a pop music TV show called *Oh Boy.* But then he'd suffered some legal difficulties in England and had found refuge in Hamburg, performing first for Bruno Koschmider and then, like the Beatles, moving up to the Top Ten. The Beatles liked Tony Sheridan personally and professionally and were quite happy with the arrangement. But as George said, "We were always looking for the next thing, thinking if only we could get a *recording.*"

As luck would have it, one night in early May Bert Kaempfert took in their show on the Reeperbahn. Kaempfert was a native Hamburger, born in the city in 1923. He had studied music in Hamburg and had performed for North German radio during World War II. By 1961 he had worked as a producer for Polydor Records for several years and had also recorded, with his own orchestra, a song he had written called "Wonderland by Night," which was destined to reach number one on the record charts in the United States. A few years later, his "Strangers in the Night" would become a huge hit for Frank Sinatra. That night in May 1961, Bert Kaempfert was so impressed with what he heard at the Top Ten that he invited Tony Sheridan and the Beatles to record for his label, Polydor.

From June 22 to 24, Kaempfert recorded the Beatles by themselves doing "Ain't She Sweet," with John on lead vocal, and an instrumental tune credited to Lennon and Harrison called "Cry for a Shadow." But the record that would have the greatest immediate impact on the life of the band was a single with "My Bonnie Lies Over the Ocean" on one side and "When the Saints Go Marching In" on the other. Kaempfert decided that nobody in the German record-buying public would know or care who the Beatles were, so the performers on the disc were identified as Tony Sheridan and the Beat Brothers. (Another reason for the temporary name change is that Kaempfert thought that "Beatles" sounded a bit too much like *peedles,* a German slang expression for the male genitalia.) Years later, the record would be reissued as "The Beatles with Tony Sheridan," but it is one of the many fateful and ironic aspects of their story that the band that would be lauded for recording their own superb songs would get their start by anonymously performing a child's nursery rhyme by an unknown author. John Lennon was very dismissive of the effort, saying contemptuously, "It's just Tony Sheridan singing, with us banging in the background. It's terrible. It could be anybody." But four months later, when the single of "My Bonnie" and "The Saints" was released as Polydor Records NH24673, that banging would have profound repercussions.

Meanwhile, the Beat Brothers continued to perform under their real name at the Top Ten. But by the end of their second stint in Hamburg they would lose a brother. Stuart Sutcliffe, who had never had any real ambitions as a musician, announced to the others that he intended to stay in Hamburg, devote all his energies to the study and practice of painting, and marry Astrid. Paul agreed to take over Stu's bass, and the Beatles' sound was now set: two guitars supported by bass and drums. Their look was slowly evolving as well. Although Stu and Astrid had introduced them to leather and their new hairstyle the previous fall, it was in the spring of 1961 that those influences really took hold. Astrid took them to a tailor who made them complete leather outfits of jackets and trousers. They found a shop that sold, as George remembered it, "genuine Texas cowboy boots. So that became our band uniform: cowboy boots and black leather suits."

The Beatles concluded their run at the Top Ten without any burned condoms or other infractions and returned to Liverpool, minus Stu, on July 3. Three days later—on the fourth anniversary of the day John met Paul—a man named Bill Harry, a former student at the Liverpool Art College who had introduced Stu Sutcliffe to John Lennon, published the first issue of *Mersey Beat*, a newsletter about the local music scene that would become hugely influential. That first issue carried John's witty discourse "On the Dubious Origins of Beatles." The second issue, two weeks later, carried a picture of the Beatles on the cover and, inside, an article about their Hamburg recording sessions with Tony Sheridan. *Mersey Beat* had already found an eager readership among Liverpool's young music enthusiasts, a popularity that was not lost on the savvy owner of the city's largest record store. So Brian Epstein promptly ordered twelve dozen copies to sell.

Brian's grandfather, Isaac Epstein, fled Poland during the pogroms at the end of the nineteenth century and settled in Liverpool, where he established a chain of highly successful furniture stores. His father, Harry Epstein, continued in the family business and quite naturally expected that his eldest son would carry on the line. But Brian Epstein, born on September 19, 1934, was a huge disappointment. Although he was brought up in relative luxury in a beautiful five-bedroom house in the fashionable Liverpool suburb of Childwall, his academic record was as dismal as John Lennon's. He was expelled from his first private school at age ten for drawing obscene pictures, although his doting mother strongly suspected that his expulsion was motivated by anti-Semitism. In the next five years Epstein attended, and unhappily departed from, six more schools. Drafted into the army in 1952, he was subsequently discharged for what were delicately termed "psychiatric grounds." Brian Epstein was gay.

He returned to Liverpool to work in a branch of the family furniture shops, but he hated the work. He began attending performances of the Liverpool Playhouse and befriended several of the actors, including a young man named Brian Bedford. Encouraged by Bedford, Brian Epstein auditioned for the Royal Academy of Dramatic Arts in London, one of the leading acting conservatories in the world. He was accepted and attended RADA for three terms, dropping out after an arrest for soliciting sex in a public park. By that time, he had already decided that he did not really like acting that much. Brian sadly went home to Liverpool to meet his destiny.

I. Epstein & Sons, the furniture stores, had expanded to include a series of shops called North End Music Stores, or NEMS, which sold sheet music, instruments, and records. Harry Epstein had just opened a new branch of NEMS in Liverpool's city center, on Great Charlotte Street. Brian took charge of the record department and, for the first time in his life, discovered something about which he could be passionate. Under his management, the Great Charlotte NEMS soon boasted pop and classical collections that rivaled those of any record shop north of London. Within two years NEMS had expanded again, to Whitechapel, just around the corner from the old fruit and vegetable district. To celebrate the new store's grand opening, Brian arranged for an in-store appearance by the actor and singer Anthony Newley. The event drew an immense crowd. Brian became something of a music celebrity in Liverpool, and when *Mersey Beat* appeared on the scene he began writing a column in which he recommended new recordings. Anthony Newley was one of his favorite artists, along with Frank Sinatra, Beatrice Lilly, and Jean Sibelius.

In his autobiography, *A Cellarful of Noise* (which John Lennon once cruelly remarked should have been called *A Cellarful of Boys*), Brian Epstein claimed that he had never heard of the Beatles when, in late October 1961, a young man came into the NEMS shop in Whitechapel asking for the new Polydor single of "My Bonnie Lies Over the Ocean." Shortly thereafter, so the story went, two girls asked for the same record, and Brian was intrigued enough to order several copies and also to begin making inquiries around town about this band called the Beatles. To his surprise, Brian discovered that not only were the Beatles English (not German), but they were from Liverpool and regularly performed at a place called the Cavern, whose entrance was two hundred yards from his shop in Whitechapel. It makes for a nice tale, but it's probably not true . . . at least the part about Brian's never having heard of the Beatles before.

After all, Brian had been writing for *Mersey Beat* and stocking the paper at NEMS for three months already. The Beatles had been on the cover, and their exploits had been extensively chronicled within its pages. At one point, a *Mersey Beat* writer had enthused, "The Beatles were the stuff that screams were made of. Here was the excitement, both physical and aural, that symbolized the rebellion of youth. Truly a phenomenon. . . . Such are the fantastic

Beatles. I don't think anything like them will happen again." It's hard to believe that with such ardor in the air that summer, and with the Cavern Club so close by, where patrons would giggle and jostle for tickets, Brian Epstein had to wait for a customer to bring the Beatles to his attention—especially when the band on "My Bonnie" was identified as the Beat Brothers.

But what is certain is that on November 9, 1961, Brian and his assistant Alistair Taylor paid a visit to the Cavern to hear the Beatles at one of their lunchtime sets. Amidst all the noise and heat and uncontrolled hormones, there sat Mr. Epstein in a proper pinstriped suit. He recalled being put off by the Beatles' raucous behavior onstage—eating and smoking and bantering with customers—but also being very taken with the excitement the band generated and with what he called their "personal magnetism." "I was fascinated by them," he said. There was probably a certain amount of extramusical attraction going on as well, with the boys' leather outfits playing no small part.

Brian returned to the Cavern to see the band several more times over the next few weeks before approaching the Beatles to propose that he become their manager. They were sorely in need of direction, as they had jettisoned Allan Williams during their second visit to Hamburg (leaving him to advise Brian bitterly that he shouldn't touch them with a bargepole), and they were favorably impressed by Brian's wealth, contacts, and relative maturity. With the under-standing that their main interest was securing a recording contract, the Beatles met Brian Epstein at the Casbah Club in early December to formalize their agreement. "I was talking to him, trying to beat him down, knowing the game, try to get the manager to take a low percentage," remembered Paul. "And the others tried as well, but he stuck at a figure of 25 per cent. He told us, 'That'll do, now I'll be your manager,' and we agreed. With my dad's advice—I remember Dad had said to get a Jewish manager—it all fitted and Brian Epstein became our manager."

Brian certainly hit the ground running. Immediately, he doubled the Beatles' fee at the Cavern, from seven and a half to fifteen pounds a night. Within days, Brian talked one of his contacts—Mike Smith, an A&R man from Decca—into hearing the band at the Cavern. Smith came away so impressed that he invited the Beatles to London for an audition on New Year's Day 1962. Brian went ahead by train. On New Year's Eve the four band members squeezed their equipment into a van driven by Neil Aspinall and, after getting lost briefly somewhere in the Midlands, made their way down the motorway to London.

It was the first time the Beatles had visited the great city, and even though they had an important engagement in the morning, they had no intention of missing out on that night's festivities in Trafalgar Square and Soho. They fell into their hotel beds at 4:30 A.M. and managed to get to the Decca studios in West Hampstead well after the appointed time of ten the next morning. Brian was already there, of course, livid that his new charges were late. "You could always tell when Brian was angry because he would undo his tie," said Pete Best. "This was definitely an undone tie moment." As luck would have it, Mike Smith had also celebrated the arrival of the New Year with gusto and came rolling into the studios a good half-hour late himself.

Over the next two hours, the Beatles performed fifteen songs, including only two Lennon-McCartney originals. Epstein wanted to demonstrate their versatility, so he recommended they perform mostly covers. Unfortunately, the band was nervous and didn't put on their best show. Paul sang Meredith Willson's "Till There Was You," but his voice quavered and cracked and he needed several takes just to get through the song. Knowing how unsettling and difficult those two hours were for the Beatles puts a new emphasis on John's offhand remark at the end of the *Let It Be* album: "We'd just like to say thanks on behalf of the band and ourselves and we hope we pass the audition!"

Mike Smith ushered the Beatles out of the studio in time to hold an audition later that same afternoon with Brian Poole and the Tremeloes. After some weeks went by and Brian still had heard nothing, he called Decca and was famously told, "Guitar groups are on the way out, Mr. Epstein. You'd better stick to selling records in Liverpool."

Contributing to the Beatles' chagrin was the knowledge that Mike Smith had been more impressed with the Tremeloes' audition than with theirs and had decided to sign that other English group to a recording contract. The Tremeloes would have a couple of hits with "Here Comes My Baby" and "Silence Is Golden," but Smith and his boss at Decca, Dick Rowe, never lived down their choice. Within two years, Paul was able to say of Rowe, with immense satisfaction, "He must be kicking himself now." To which John responded, "I hope he kicks himself to death."

The pain of Decca's decision was slightly offset by the news that a new *Mersey Beat* poll had shown the Beatles to be the most popular band in Liverpool, leading the second-place Gerry and the Pacemakers by five thousand votes. The Beatles were now clearly in a class by themselves in the north of England. Unfortunately, even as their touring increased, Brian's pile of rejection letters from record labels kept growing; Pye, Philips, Columbia, and EMI all agreed with Decca in saying no. On the road with Neil Aspinall, to gigs in Manchester, Wolverhampton, Swindon, and Crewe, the boys kept their spirits up through a repeated routine. John would shout, "Where are we going, fellas?" The other three would bellow back, "To the top, Johnny!" "What top?" John would ask, and the response was always, "To the toppermost of the poppermost, Johnny!" They all still believed in their golden future.

If a recording seemed to be in the distant future, however, another medium quickly embraced them. On March 8, 1962, the Beatles made their radio debut on the BBC Light Programme *Teenagers Turn—Here We Go*. Their performances, which included three covers— "Dream Baby," "Please Mr. Postman," and "Memphis, Tennessee"—were actually recorded the previous day before a live audience at the Playhouse Theatre in Manchester. At the time of the broadcast, the boys gathered at the Casbah Club back home in Liverpool to listen and cheer. Their national audience had grown instantly, and their local audience was about to notice a radical change in their appearance.

From his first sight of them down in the Cavern, Brian

Epstein thought that the Beatles needed smartening up. Almost immediately he began sending them little notes about their stage deportment ("Note that during the performances smoking, eating, chewing, and drinking is STRICTLY PROHIBITED") and the importance of punctuality. Then, drawing upon his stage background, he determined that the boys needed a new, cleaner look to attract a wider audience. He instructed them to wear suits and ties on stage and to execute a simultaneous bow after each song. The Beatles resisted a bit at first, particularly John and Pete, but they all came around when they realized that their careers could benefit. A few years later John said, a bit defensively, "Brian wasn't trying to clean our image up; he said our look wasn't right, we'd never get past the door at a good place. It was a choice of making it or still eating chicken on stage. We respected his views."

The new look debuted at the Cavern on April 5, at a show presented by the recently organized Beatles Fan Club. The band played in their familiar black leather Hamburg attire during the first half of the concert and then came out after intermission in their suits and ties. Each attending fan was presented with a picture of the band sporting the suit look, to reinforce what Brian hoped was a good first impression.

Less than a week later, the Beatles returned for a third visit to Hamburg. And they returned in style, by air, a far cry from their first arrival nearly two years before. They were looking forward to the trip for both professional and personal reasons. They would play the new Star Club, Hamburg's biggest venue on the Reeperbahn, and they would share the bill with one of their heroes, Gene Vincent. And they would be reunited with Stu Sutcliffe.

But they landed at Hamburg Airport on April 11 to meet an anguished Astrid Kirchherr, who brokenly informed them that Stu was dead. He'd been suffering excruciating headaches for months, along with double vision and violent mood swings. On April 10 he was stricken with a brain hemorrhage; he was rushed to a hospital but died in Astrid's arms in the ambulance. He was twenty-one years old. An autopsy revealed that his skull had received a trau-matic blow that had caused a shock to his brain. It's most likely that the beating he'd absorbed at the Litherland Town Hall two years before was the source of that trauma.

The Beatles were crushed, especially John. "It was the first time that I'd seen John cry," said Pete Best. "He just broke down and sobbed." Later, when the band returned to Liverpool, John asked Mrs. Sutcliffe for the long scarf that Stu had worn when the two boys had met at art college. But the show in Hamburg had to go on, and the Beatles were unhappy headliners for the next seven weeks.

Brian had accompanied the Beatles to Germany, but after a week he returned to England to resume his determined quest to land his band a record deal. Although the audition at Decca had come to naught, he had secured the tapes of the sessions, and it was these reels that he was using to shop the Beatles around. It occured to him that it might be more convenient for record executives to have 78 rpm discs to listen to, so he went to the huge HMV Shop on London's Oxford Street to have the tapes transferred. The man who ran the operation liked what he heard, and when Brian told him that the Beatles also wrote and performed their own songs, he suggested that Brian meet with Sid Coleman, the director of EMI's publishing company. On May 8, while the boys were still in Hamburg, Brian played his new 78s for Coleman, who in turn was so impressed that he arranged a meeting with a friend who produced recordings for Parlophone, a division of EMI. The producer's name was George Martin.

In 1962, George Martin was thirty-six and had been the head of Parlophone for seven years, since the day Sir Joseph Lockwood appointed him the youngest man to direct a label for EMI. Although he hailed from North London, the son of a carpenter, Martin spoke with the quiet, clipped, authoritative voice of a BBC newsreader, which in fact he had been. He also could point to a solid musical background. He had been the pianist and leader of his own dance band, George Martin and the Four Tune Tellers; he had studied music at the prestigious Guildhall School, concentrating on conducting, composition, orchestration, music theory, and piano performance; and he had learned the oboe well enough to freelance his way through several jobs with London's many orchestras. As a record producer he'd worked with classical musicians, jazz artists, and comedians, including Peter Ustinov, Flanders and Swann, and the mad trio of Peter Sellers, Spike Milligan, and Harry Secombe, better known as the Goons. On May 9, George Martin welcomed Brian Epstein into his office, listened to the five-month-old Decca session, and promptly offered a provisional recording contract, provided that the Beatles could pass another audition, set for

June 6. Elated, Brian dashed off a telegram to the Beatles in Hamburg: "Congratulations, boys. EMI request recording session. Please rehearse new material." Brian was so pleased and proud of this accomplishment that he kept a copy of the telegram as a talisman for the rest of his life.

Over the next month the Beatles did indeed work some new material into their shows at the Star Club, including a Lennon-McCartney original called "Love Me Do." That new song was one of four that the Beatles recorded during their audition with George Martin on June 6 at EMI's legendary Abbey Road studios in London's posh St. John's Wood. They also recorded two other Lennon-McCartney pieces, "P.S. I Love You" and "Ask Me Why," as well as a Latin standard called "Besame Mucho" that they had also performed for Mike Smith at Decca. George Martin recalled later that he was immediately drawn to the boys' personalities and saw their potential, but that he had some doubts about Pete Best's drumming and determined that, if he were to sign the band, he would see about securing the services of a session drummer for studio work.

Martin also expressed some reservations about the Beatles' original songs, fearing that they didn't have what it took to climb the charts. As a remedy, he suggested they learn a song by Mitch Murray called "How Do You Do It?" which he felt sure would become a number-one hit. The boys nodded, a little dazed by the whole experience, and left Abbey Road not knowing whether they would ever return.

At the end of June they participated in the last concert

held at the Casbah Club, which they had opened nearly three years before. Mona Best had recently separated from her husband, John, and had taken up with the Beatles' road manager, Neil Aspinall. She and Neil were expecting a child in July. So the Casbah, the first real home the Beatles had enjoyed, closed its doors for forty-one years, until it reopened in 2003 as a shrine to fans from around the world.

In late July, while the Beatles maintained a nearly nightly schedule of performances at such venues as Liverpool's Cavern Club, the Majestic Ballroom in Birkenhead, the Hulme Hall Golf Club, and the Automatic Telephone Company's Royal Iris River Cruise, Brian Epstein received the electrifying news that George Martin wanted the band to sign a contract with Parlophone Records. They were due back at Abbey Road for a recording session on September 4. Brian excitedly told John, who passed the word on to Paul and George. Nobody told Pete.

On Wednesday night, August 15, the Beatles played the Cavern. They were scheduled to play in Chester on the sixteenth, and Pete and John planned to drive over together. As they were leaving the Cavern on Wednesday, Pete asked John what time he should pick him up the next day. John mumbled something noncommittal and rushed off, leaving Pete with the distinct impression that something was up. Summoned to Brian's office at NEMS the next day, Pete learned the awful truth: the others wanted him out and Ringo Starr in. They couldn't face him with the news and left it to their manager to wield the knife.

There were apparently several reasons for the firing of

Pete Best. He never really fit in with the other three, he was a bit of a loner, he didn't want to change his hairstyle, he was unreliable, and, probably most significantly, he was a below-average drummer. After the Beatles broke up in 1970, John said, "Pete was a bit slow. He was a harmless guy, but he was not quick. All of us had quick minds but he never picked that up. The reason he got into the group in the first place was because we had to have a drummer to get to Hamburg. We were always going to dump him when we could find a decent drummer but by the time we got back from Germany we'd trained him to keep a stick going up and down, and he looked nice and the girls liked him so it was all right. But we were cowards when we sacked him."

George recalled, "To me it was apparent. Pete kept being sick and not showing up for gigs so we would get Ringo to sit in with the band instead and every time Ringo sat in it seemed like 'this is it.' Eventually we realized, 'We should get Ringo in the band full time.'" John called Ringo and offered him the job at a salary of twenty-five pounds a week. Ringo had just received an offer to join Kingsize Taylor and the Dominoes for twenty pounds a week. So he took the extra five quid, and fame and fortune followed.

Pete was deeply shocked, and his mother, Mona, was bitter. "I'd looked upon them as friends," she said, speaking of John, Paul, and George. "I'd helped them so much, got them bookings, lent them money. I fed them when they were hungry. I was far more interested in them than their own parents." But as angry as Mona was in

1962, by 1967 she had forgiven John to the extent that she loaned him her father's old army medals to pin to his bright lemon-lime uniform for the cover of *Sgt. Pepper's Lonely Hearts Club Band*.

No such forgiveness was in the hearts of Pete Best's many fans, who flocked to the Cavern on August 19 for the Beatles' first hometown performance with their new drummer. Many of them chanted the slogan "Pete Best forever, Ringo never!" or "Pete is Best!" A few punches were thrown, and George Harrison, believed by some to be the ringleader in Pete's ouster, received a black eye. Through the maelstrom sat Ringo, his head nodding left and right in what would become his signature gesture, secure in his new position. "I never felt sorry for Pete Best. I was not involved," he said later. "Besides, I felt I was a much better drummer than he was."

There's no doubt that he was. But who of us who has ever felt betrayed or deprived of a prize we felt was rightfully ours cannot imagine the many endless nights that lay ahead for Pete Best?

Later that week, John got married. His wife was Cynthia Powell, a girl from across the Mersey in Hoylake, whom he had met in art college. From the early days of the Quarry Men, through the Moondogs and the Silver Beatles and the long nights on the Reeperbahn, John and Cynthia had carried on a sometimes chaotic, often passionate, always demanding relationship. In midsummer of 1962 Cynthia announced that she was pregnant, and John dutifully agreed to marriage. The ceremony took place on August 23 at Mount Pleasant Register Office in

Liverpool. His aunt Mimi, furious at the turn of events, boycotted the wedding. Paul and George attended, wearing black. A construction jackhammer in the street outside made it nearly impossible to hear what the officiant was saying. "Then," said John, "we went across the road and had a chicken dinner. I can't remember any presents. But I did feel embarrassed being married. Walking about, married. It was like walking about with odd socks on, your fly open." John spent his wedding night onstage at the Riverpark Ballroom in Chester. All in all, it wasn't a promising beginning to a marriage.

Less than eight months later, on April 8, 1963, John and Cynthia's son, Julian Lennon, was born. The fact that one of the Beatles was married and had a child presented an awkward dilemma to Brian Epstein, who feared that such news might harm the group's image with some of their female fans. So Cynthia and Julian were effectively hidden from public view for years.

The Lennon-McCartney originals "Love Me Do" and "P.S. I Love You" were the focus of the Beatles' first-ever recording sessions, which took place at the Abbey Road studios on September 4 and 11. Having heard that Pete Best had been replaced, George Martin did not carry out his threat to hire a session drummer—at first. Ringo played drums on "Love Me Do" and on "How Do You Do It?" (the Mitch Murray song that Martin had asked them to learn) on the fourth, but when the band returned a week later, Ringo was shocked and dismayed to discover session drummer Andy White sitting at the drum set ready to go. Ringo was handed a tambourine and a set of maracas to play, and he was sure that after the session he would be handed his walking papers as well. But the rest of the Beatles persuaded Martin that Ringo was the answer.

The Beatles took another stand during those sessions—a stand crucial to establishing their signature sound and, more important, their integrity as an ensemble. It was established convention that songwriters, music publishers, and record producers, all working together, would simply instruct the musicians, usually dismissively referred to as "the talent," to play whatever was put in front of them. That was the context in which George Martin had asked the Beatles to record "How Do You Do It?" But they insisted that the song just wasn't them. George Harrison called it "corny," and Paul declared that they couldn't go back up to Liverpool and face their fans and fellow musicians with that song attached to their names. George Martin deeply believed that "How Do You Do It?" was a potential number-one song. But in the face of a firm opinion expressed by a seasoned producer speaking in the venerable home of EMI, the four young men, the oldest of them barely twenty-two, stood their ground. It would be their songs that would introduce them to the world.

To his credit, George Martin understood and agreed to issue, as the Beatles' first single, "Love Me Do" and "P.S. I Love You." But he also revealed his skills as a producer and judge of material. The Beatles played him another Lennon-McCartney original called "Please Please Me" that they had in mind for their next single. It was in the manner of a Roy Orbison ballad, slow and deliberate. Martin did not like their version at all, calling it "dreary," and suggested that they relearn it at a faster tempo in time for their next recording session. He gave "How Do You Do It?" to another Liverpool band, Gerry and the Pacemakers; just as Martin had predicted, their record made it to the top of the charts.

"Love Me Do," backed by "P.S. I Love You," was released on October 5. It wasn't a smash hit by any means, but it reached number seventeen and gave the boys an immense kick. "First hearing 'Love Me Do' on the radio sent me shivery all over," said George. "It was the best buzz of all time."

A week later the Beatles met one of their idols. Richard Wayne Penniman, the flamboyant rocker known as Little Richard, joined them for a monster concert at the Tower Ballroom in Wallasey. Also on the bill were Billy J. Kramer, Rory Storm and the Hurricanes, the Merseybeats, and—probably uncomfortably for all concerned—Lee Curtis and the All Stars, including the group's new drummer, Pete Best. The Beatles were thrilled to meet Little Richard—"We were almost paralysed with adoration," said John—and the enthusiasm went both ways. "Man, those Beatles are fabulous," Richard raved. "If I hadn't seen them I'd never have known they were white. They have a real authentic Negro sound." At the end of the month, the Beatles were reunited with Little Richard for a two-week engagement at the Star Club in Hamburg, their fourth visit to the city that had meant so much to their development.

On November 26, they returned to the Abbey Road

studios to record their second single. They'd taken George Martin's advice and speeded up "Please Please Me," but their producer now had two more good suggestions that the Beatles took to heart. Martin felt that since John's harmonica had been such an integral part of the sonic texture of "Love Me Do," it should make an immediate appearance at the top of their next record, and it helps kick off "Please Please Me" with a bright, edgy exuberance. Martin also devised the rapid-fire chords that underlie the stratospheric voices of John and Paul at the close. The song lasts all of one minute and fifty-nine seconds, but the excitement and ebulliance of the music is intoxicating, and everyone in the studio sensed it immediately. John said proudly, "We were so happy with the result, we couldn't get it recorded fast enough." At the end of the sessions, Martin announced over the studio intercom, "Boys, you've just made your first Number One!"

Released on January 11, 1963, with "Ask Me Why" on the B side, the record started climbing the charts slowly but steadily. Brian sent them out on the road, opening for a teenage singing star named Helen Shapiro. The tour took them to such cities as Gloucester and Carlisle, Coventry and Taunton, Exeter and Sheffield and Hull. On February 22, in Manchester, the band learned that "Please Please Me" had fulfilled George Martin's expectation, reaching the number-one position on the national sales charts. The Beatles had indeed gone to the toppermost of the poppermost, but they—and the world—were about to discover realms beyond the poppermost, Johnny.

6

"O Come All Ye Faithful, Yeah, Yeah, Yeah!"

"It was never an overnight success," points out Paul McCartney. "It started in pubs, we went on to talent contests and then to working man's clubs. We played Hamburg clubs, and then we started to play town halls and night clubs, and then ballrooms. Next up from that was theatres. . . . When we began to headline bills on theatres, we felt we had really arrived. The next ladder to climb was radio. It was a gentle thing; we had conquered the clubs—we'd conquered the Indra, we'd conquered the Cavern—and we had gradually become quite known, so it was, 'Well, what's left? Radio!'"

Radio and television came calling on the Beatles in 1963, helping to forge an image of ubiquity that year. Suddenly they seemed to be everywhere—on the airwaves, in the newspapers and magazines, and still very much on the road, performing for young audiences who, more and more, demonstrated just why the word *fan* derives from *fanatic*.

In the first weeks of 1963, the Beatles appeared on a Scottish TV program called *Round-Up,* the English Alpha TV show *Thank Your Lucky Stars,* and the Granada TV program *People and Places.* They also became regulars on BBC radio, showing up on *Here We Go, Saturday Club* (a program hosted by Brian Matthew that Paul had listened to faithfully while lying in bed on Saturday mornings on Forthlin Road), *Side by Side, Pop Inn,* and *Steppin' Out.* They even performed "Please Please Me" with a glove puppet, Lenny the Lion, on the BBC children's television program *Pops and Lenny.*

After the Helen Shapiro tour, the Beatles went out on the road again, this time with Chris Montez and Tommy Roe, and a little later with another of their idols, Roy Orbison. It was Orbison's style that John was trying to copy with his first version of "Please Please Me." Even though the Beatles headlined the show, and thus went on after Orbison, they always regarded following him on stage as very heavy lifting. "It was terrible following him," said Ringo. "He'd slay them and they'd scream for more. He was just doing it with his voice. Just standing there singing, not moving or anything. He was knocking them out. As it got near our turn, we would hide behind the curtain, whispering to each other—guess who's next, folks."

But the Beatles inspired their own share of screaming. The crowds back home at the Cavern had been very enthusiastic, but now the adulation came pitched a little higher and began to include a touch of hysteria, with their primarily young and female fans shrieking at the first sound of a song. George happened to mention to an inquiring reporter that he had a fondness for jelly beans, and their stage shows now included the obbligato "ping" of jelly beans landing on the stage, on Ringo's drums, or—less noisily but more painfully—on the boys themselves. Pandemonium became an expected component of their concerts and of their mad dashes to and from halls and hotels. Young women often stationed themselves strategically outside to reap the rewards. "If you could quickly suss out the ones who looked half decent," said an appreciative George, "you could push them in through the door with you, slam it behind, and then they'd come up to the room. . . ."

The fuel for it all was their music, and the Beatles and George Martin decided it was time to provide their fans with long-playing petrol. In 1963 pop music was measured out in singles, 45-rpm discs that came wrapped in flimsy paper sleeves and were cheap enough to accommodate the average teenager's allowance. Albums were generally reserved for Broadway shows or collections of standards sung by the likes of Frank Sinatra or Ella Fitzgerald. The Beatles were already mold breakers by being a group in which all four members sang (rather than a leader with three backup singers), and by performing their own songs. With their first $33\frac{1}{3}$ rpm album, the Beatles began to change the way popular music was recorded, marketed, listened to, and regarded.

They walked into Abbey Road's Studio Two at ten

o'clock on the morning of February 11, 1963, and they stumbled out twelve hours later having recorded an album. "One, two, three, FAH!" counts off Paul, as the band rocks into "I Saw Her Standing There" and kicks off their magnificent LP legacy. The album *Please Please Me* contains eight Lennon-McCartney originals, although it's interesting to note that the songs are credited to "McCartney/Lennon" on the back of the record. They include a song that John wrote for George, "Do You Want to Know a Secret?" which was inspired by a line uttered by Jiminy Cricket in the Walt Disney movie *Pinocchio*.

George Martin's concept for the album was to try to reproduce the flavor of a Beatles concert, including some of their many cover songs. Arthur Alexander, the Shirelles, and the teams of Gerry Goffin and Carole King and Bobby Scott and Ric Marlow were the sources of five of the covers. The album ended with one of the Beatles' signature performances, their version of the Phil Medley–Bert Russell barnburner "Twist and Shout," previously recorded by the Isley Brothers. Knowing what a taxing song it is to sing, Martin left it for the very end of the all-day session.

Although "Twist and Shout" came early in the Beatles' recording history, very little they did in the next seven years topped its urgency, power, musicality, suggestiveness, and raw fun. It is the essence of great rock 'n' roll and it stands on John's amazing lead vocal. Concluding twelve hours of work, "Twist and Shout" "nearly killed me," said John. "My voice wasn't the same for a long time after; every time I swallowed it was like sandpaper." It was worth it, for us, anyway—John shredded his larynx for a very good cause that night.

The cover photograph for *Please Please Me* was taken by Angus McBean, looking up at the Beatles as they peered smilingly down over a balcony at EMI's offices in London's Manchester Square, the four of them dressed in matching brown suits. It was a pose they reproduced six years later for two albums of greatest hits—the so-called Red and Blue albums. The change in the boys' outward appearance was a silent but powerful—and today, poignant—summation of how much the world had turned in that time.

The same day that photograph was taken, March 5, the Beatles recorded their third single. On the tour bus with Helen Shapiro a few weeks earlier, John and Paul were flipping through the pages of the *New Musical Express* to see how their records were doing in the NME Chart and noticed that the Letters to the Editor column was headlined "From You to Us." With that friendly sentiment as their inspiration, the two put their heads together and, as the bus rolled west from York to Shrewsbury, wrote down, "If there's anything that you want, if there's anything I can do, just call on me and I'll send it along with love from me to you." "From Me to You," with the B Side "Thank You Girl," was released on April 11. Like the Beatles' previous single, it, too, reached number one, although it took far less time to get there, a mere two weeks. It sold well over five hundred thousand copies by the end of the summer.

Meanwhile, the *Please Please Me* album, released on March 22, quickly ascended to the top spot on the British

LP charts and stayed there for thirty weeks. Today, of course, we're accustomed to the idea of Beatles hits, but in the spring of 1963 it was an amazing accomplishment for an unknown band from Liverpool to have two singles and an album demonstrate such dominance. There was a built-in condescension toward the North in English social and artistic circles at the time that was every bit as pervasive as condescension toward the South here in America. The success of such Northern actors as Albert Finney and Brian Bedford had begun to break down those barriers of prejudice, but the coming of the Beatles was a stick of dynamite.

"We were told all the time, 'You'll never do anything, you Northern bastards,'" said George. "It was that kind of attitude. So the first thing we did on 'making it' was to give [the finger] to all those bands who started out with a much better chance than us because they were from London."

With the recordings in the can, the Helen Shapiro tour behind them, and the Roy Orbison tour looming in May, the Beatles took a brief break in April. Paul, George, and Ringo flew to Tenerife in the Canary Islands, staying in a house owned by the parents of Klaus Voormann, whom they'd met in Hamburg. They stayed for a dozen days, snorkeling, getting sunburned, and reveling in the restful Spanish atmosphere. Paul got caught in a riptide one afternoon and almost drowned, but all in all it was a peaceful release from what had become a grueling schedule.

While the other three were cavorting in the Canaries, John left Cynthia, who'd just given birth to Julian, and traveled to Torremolinos, Spain, in the ardent company of

Brian Epstein. "Brian was in love with me," said John many years later. "It's irrelevant. I mean, it's interesting and it will make a nice Hollywood Babylon some day about Brian Epstein's sex life, but it's absolutely irrelevant." What may or may not have occurred between John and Brian in Spain is both irrelevant and unknown, but it occasioned violence a few weeks later at Paul's twenty-first-birthday party. Bob Wooler, a Liverpool disc jockey, started plying John with insinuating questions about the supposed "love affair," and John beat him up. He broke three of Wooler's ribs and later paid him two hundred pounds as restitution. The story appeared on the back page of the *Daily Mirror* (ironically, the first coverage the Beatles received from the national press), but fortunately for all it quickly died.

In many ways, that incident was a way station in John's life and in the life of the band. So shaken was he by his own rage (brought on, he said, by drink and fear of what his true sexual orientation might be) that he vowed to turn away from the fighting and anger that had been so much a part of his earlier days. At about the same time, the Beatles, much to the dismay of their original devoted fans, began to spend less and less time in their hometown. Paul had just met Jane Asher, a bright and accomplished actress and radio personality who hailed from a prominent London family. He moved in with the Ashers and lived in their lovely home on Wimpole Street for two years. On August 3, 1963, the Beatles played their last concert at the Cavern on Liverpool's Mathew Street. They had outgrown its dank and dark confines and were playing commodious theaters with orchestra seats and balconies. They now belonged to all of England and soon would be claimed by the whole world.

In the summer of 1963 the band began appearing regularly on a BBC radio program called *Pop Go the Beatles*. The show was recorded a few days before broadcast at the BBC's Aeolian Hall studios in London. On fifteen Tuesday evenings at five o'clock, the show opened with a rock 'n' roll version of "Pop Goes the Weasel" performed by the Beatles, then the announcer Rodney Burke would warble, "It's five o'clock, we're ready to pop. It's the 'Pop Go the Beatles' spot!" Every week the Beatles would play (and talk about, sometimes seriously, often hilariously) five songs from their vast repertoire. By September they'd performed fifty-six different songs by such artists as Chuck Berry, Carl Perkins, Arthur Crudup, Goffin and King, Lieber and Stoller, and, occasionally, Lennon and McCartney. Twenty-five of those songs were not released on albums and would remain locked in the vast BBC vaults until they appeared on CD in 1994.

As big as the Beatles had become, they were about to become even bigger, almost unimaginably big. On July 1, once again in Studio Two at Abbey Road, they recorded their fourth single, the anthemic, totemic, toe-tapping "She Loves You," the song that so evokes the essence of early Beatlemania that the Beatles twice quoted it in later songs. It's a sincere piece of advice from one man to another as he tries to patch up what could become a relationship-ending quarrel between his friend and the friend's girlfriend. The first man acknowledges the fear, the guilt, and the stubborn pride that the rift has wrought but brings good news: despite everything, she loves you, and (by implication, you stupid jerk), you know you should be very glad about that. So stop being a jerk and make up! In many ways, those are the words of a Sensitive New Age Guy thirty years ahead of his time.

To underscore just how serious he is, our SNAG follows up his insistence that his friend is loved with emphatic repetitions of the word *yeah*. It was dismissed as a simple nonsense hook by older critics and embraced as a defining idiom by their adoring fans, but "yeah, yeah, yeah" is more than either. It's an early and joyous affirmation of the band's abiding faith in the irreplaceable importance of love.

Paul's father, Jim, objected the first time he heard the song, complaining, "Son, there's enough Americanisms around. Couldn't you sing 'yes, yes, yes' just for once?" To which Paul replied, "You don't understand, Dad. It wouldn't work!"

The words, simple though they undoubtedly are (composed by John and Paul in a hotel room in Newcastle-upon-Tyne just four days before the recording session), are backed up by some utterly dynamic music. Ringo's drums seem to be tumbling downstairs at the outset, giving way to the Beatles' definitive ringing guitars and insistent vocal lines that alternate between unison and harmony. The song ends with George contributing his voice to a stunning three-part sixth chord. George Martin advised against it, saying that the chord sounded too old-fashioned. But the Beatles insisted, once again proving their integrity and their instincts. As a final stroke that would forever confer an unmistakable originality on the song, John and Paul twice leaned into the microphones, shook their heads, and wailed "Wooo!" It drove the fans wild; it also expressed the joy and hopeful abandon that remains a hallmark of the Beatles' sound and ensures their immortality.

Since the day in June when word leaked out that another Beatles single was on the way, record stores had been taking orders for it. By August 23, the date of its release, more than a half million copies of the record had already been presold. It went gold, signifying a million copies sold, on October 11. Quickly taking over the number-one slot in the British charts, "She Loves You" became the biggest-selling single in the country's history.

On October 13, the Beatles climbed to yet another plateau in their continuing ascent by appearing at the top of the bill on the nationally televised *Sunday Night at the London Palladium*. In some ways, that night was just another gig; the band played four of their hits, including "She Loves You" and "Twist and Shout," and shared the enormous revolving stage at the Palladium with the English entertainer Des O'Connor and the American soul singer Brook Benton. But the magnitude of the night far exceeded that of their previous appearances. Ringo recalled that long before when he was playing skiffle with Eddie Clayton, a neighbor named Annie Maguire often assured him that one day she'd see his name in lights on the Palladium marquee. Actually playing the Palladium and realizing such a long-held dream brought on so many

conflicting feelings of pride and anxiety that Ringo vom-
ited just before going out onstage.

But events inside the Palladium were only part of the
story. Outside the building, the band's fans swarmed, some
vying for tickets, others merely hoping for a glimpse of the
boys. Traffic on Argyle Street and nearby Marlborough
Street slowed to a crawl and then stopped completely.
Police attempted to disperse the crowds and found themselves attacked. Under the headline "Siege of the Beatles,"
the next day's *Daily Herald* reported that "screaming girls
launched themselves against the police, sending helmets
flying and constables reeling." But the paper also reported
the success of the concert inside, proclaiming "Love
Makes The Lads Light Up." Across Britain, fifteen million
people, the band's largest audience so far, tuned in to share
the love.

Many histories of the Beatles have dated the band's adulation by the masses, summed up by the *Daily Mirror*'s use
of the headline "Beatlemania!" from that October night.
But the scene in front of the Palladium was really just a
continuation of what had been occurring at clubs in Liverpool, Leeds, Blackpool, Bournemouth, and countless
other British cities and towns for some time already. Of
course, in the minds of solipsistic Fleet Street editors, if
it hadn't happened in London it hadn't really happened
at all, so they all felt free to announce the birth of a
phenomenon that was already several months old.

Within days came evidence that Beatlemania wasn't confined to England. On October 23, the Beatles flew to
Sweden for a week of concerts, television performances,

and personal appearances. Their arrival at Stockholm International Airport was greeted with anything but traditional Swedish reserve, as hundreds of girls who had taken off from school screamed and panted and threw flowers at the boys. The next day, newspapers described what had happened as "The Battle of Stockholm Airport."

On October 31, when the Beatles flew back to London's Heathrow Airport, an even bigger melee awaited them. Thousands of fans flocked to the roof of the Queen's Building, waving signs welcoming the boys home. Thousands more clogged the roads leading to the airport, trapping Prime Minister Sir Alec Douglas-Home inside his limousine. The reigning Miss World, expecting a sizable welcome of her own when she flew into Heathrow that day, was completely ignored. According to legend, another witness to the turmoil that day was the American showman Ed Sullivan, who immediately began making plans to introduce the Beatles to America.

There had been such breathless and rapturous coverage of the Beatles in the London papers since the Palladium show that a little backlash was probably in order. It arrived on November 2 in the form of a *Daily Telegraph* editorial voicing alarm at all the hysteria. The editorial compared the rush of emotion at Beatles concerts with the flag-draped and torch-lit drama of Hitler's rallies at Nuremburg. The *Daily Mirror* instantly defended the boys against such hyperbole, declaring, "You have to be a real sour square not to love the nutty, noisy, happy, handsome Beatles!" A fortnight later, a Church of England vicar wrote that church attendance during the coming Christmas season could be increased if the Beatles could be persuaded to record "O Come All Ye Faithful, Yeah, Yeah, Yeah!"

Few moments in the band's rocket to stardom that autumn could match John's remark at the end of the Beatles' appearance at the Royal Command Performance on Monday night, November 4. The annual event, held in 1963 at the staid Prince of Wales Theatre in London, was a curious commingling of artists and society types who tended to regard the performers as so many dancing bears brought together for their amusement. Patrons usually brought binoculars, which were trained equally on the stage and on the royal box, the better to judge what sort of impression the people onstage were making on the concert's key constituents. In the minds of many of the performers, it was all pretty hideous, but the ordeal usually paid off in publicity.

That night at the Prince of Wales, the Prince himself was not in attendance, but the Queen Mother, Princess Margaret, and Lord Snowden all were. The bill included Marlene Dietrich, Michael Flanders and Donald Swann, Harry Secombe (who had made records with George Martin), and quite a few more singers, dancers, comedians, and orchestra leaders. The Beatles were the seventh act to perform. They began with "From Me to You" and followed with "She Loves You." In an unusual departure from other recent Beatles performances, the very proper audience didn't scream or carry on at all, and tapes reveal the tightness of the band's playing and the beauty of harmonies so often lost amid the tumult. Perhaps there is something to be said for propriety after all.

Paul then got a chuckle from the crowd when he introduced "Till There Was You" by saying that the song had been "recorded by our favorite American group, Sophie Tucker." After his solo, John stepped up to his microphone and with the slyest of grins announced, "For our last number I'd like to ask your help. Would the people in the cheaper seats clap your hands? And the rest of you, if you'd just rattle your jewelry." With that, the Beatles swung into "Twist and Shout."

"I was fantastically nervous," John recalled years later, "but I wanted to say something to rebel a bit, and that was the best I could do." There have certainly been greater, and more effective, acts of rebellion in music history, but John's wisecrack was a telling reminder of the class differences on display that night in the Prince of Wales, and it served notice that the Beatles had abandoned neither their working-class origins nor their working-class senses of humor. The remark further endeared the boys to their like-minded listeners.

As usual, though, nothing cemented the bond between the Beatles and their fans more strongly than their music. Just after the Royal Command Performance a second album was due. Unlike *Please Please Me,* which was recorded in a single day, LP number two, *With the Beatles,* required eleven sessions, beginning with a first visit to Abbey Road on July 18 and concluding with some over-dubbing on October 23, the day they left for Sweden.

Like its predecessor, *With the Beatles* contained eight original songs and six covers. The covers included three great Motown songs, all sung magnificently by John—the

Marvelettes' "Please Mr. Postman," Smokey Robinson's "You Really Got a Hold on Me," and Barrett Strong's "Money (That's What I Want)." In addition, George sang lead on Chuck Berry's classic "Roll Over Beethoven." It is likely that more white kids were introduced to African-American music by the Beatles than by the original artists. This fact may frustrate black musicians, yet the recordings are a testament to the Beatles' devotion to this music that they loved and always credited as a major influence.

Of the originals on the new album, the highlights included John's "It Won't Be Long," which echoes the use of the word "yeah" from "She Loves You," and Paul's sweet "All My Loving." George introduced himself to the world as a solo composer with "Don't Bother Me." The album's lasting visual impression is its striking cover photograph. Remembering the shadowy photos taken of them in Hamburg by Astrid Kirchherr, the Beatles asked Robert Freeman if he could approximate that atmosphere. He responded by taking them to a hotel ballroom, drawing the thick curtains, and providing a single intense light source. Freeman then placed John, George, and Paul next to each other and asked Ringo to kneel on a chair; all four of them wore black turtlenecks. The resulting photograph was one of the most famous images of the decade: four young men whose faces were open and familiar and yet hid the impenetrable mystery of their singular talents.

When the impending release of *With the Beatles* was announced, it immediately attracted more than two hundred fifty thousand advance orders. Its actual availability prompted a delirious run on record shops as fans old and new who had followed the boys' many public appearances over the past month seized this latest incarnation of delight and exuberance. *With the Beatles* replaced *Please Please Me* as number one on the British album charts.

But by nightfall, joy had given way to heartbreak. *With the Beatles* had been released on Friday, November 22, 1963.

7

"Such a Feeling"

Even though the Beatles had been a national phenomenon in England for the better part of 1963, they were still largely unknown in America in November. By then, the band had produced four singles that had gone to number one in England—"Please Please Me," "From Me to You," "She Loves You," and "I Want to Hold Your Hand"—but Americans remained largely ignorant of them. For that they had to thank, at least in part, Dave Dexter, the director of Capitol Records, the U.S.-based popular music division of EMI.

George Martin remembers doing his best to interest his American counterparts in his work with the Beatles. "I would send each record to my friends at Capitol Records and say, 'This group is fantastic, you've got to sell them in the States.' And each time, the head of Capitol would turn it down. 'Sorry, we know our market better than you do and we don't think they're any good.'"

Since Capitol had exercised their right of first refusal, EMI contacted another American label called Vee-Jay.

Started in Gary, Indiana, in 1953, and later operating out of Chicago, Vee-Jay was named for its two owners, Vivian and James Bracken, the first African Americans to operate a large independent record company. Before the advent of Motown, the Brackens turned Vee-Jay into the most successful black-owned record company in America. Their stable of recording artists included some great doo-wop, blues, and gospel groups (the Spaniels, John Lee Hooker, the Staple Singers), but Vee-Jay also had a million-seller with Gene Chandler's "Duke of Earl" and made some recordings with the Four Seasons and Jimi Hendrix. After negotiating with EMI, the Brackens agreed to issue a big British hit, "I Remember You" by Frank Ifield, and also decided to take a chance on the Beatles. They released "Please Please Me" on February 25, 1963, and "From Me to You" on May 27. In contrast to the millions of copies sold in the UK, the Beatles' Vee-Jay singles sold fewer than ten thousand copies.

Late that summer, Dave Dexter at Capitol decided against releasing "She Loves You," so EMI went shopping again. By this time Vee-Jay Records was already involved in the sorts of financial disputes that would force the company to declare bankruptcy in 1966, so EMI made a deal with a small Philadelphia-based label called Swan Records. Swan's biggest seller up to that time had been "Palisades Park" by Freddy Cannon, and their list of artists featured such acts as Danny and the Juniors and Dicky Doo and the Don'ts. On September 15, Swan had the honor of releasing "She Loves You" in America. Dick Clark played the recording on his national *American Bandstand* TV program, but despite this enormous exposure, the single failed to break into the American charts. The record-buying and radio-listening public remained impervious to the Beatles' charms.

My parents, who owed their lives to the six years they had spent performing with an all-Jewish orchestra in Nazi Germany, had enthusiastically voted for John F. Kennedy for president in 1960 and were delighted at the parade of musicians, actors, and dancers who were now regularly invited to perform at the White House. I was a fan, too. My father had roused me early one day in the fall of 1960 to attend a Kennedy rally. My brother came as well, and afterward asked Kennedy to autograph his copy of Kennedy's Pulitzer Prize–winning book, *Profiles in Courage*. We all liked his looks, his ideals, his (in the celebrated accent that was widely parodied) *vigah*.

I remember his solemn address to the nation in October 1962, when he warned us of the terrible danger posed by Russian missiles in Cuba. I remember the quiet, somber bus ride to school the next morning, as each of us rowdy kids now sat silently, contemplating in our ten-year-old minds the end of the world. I remember Kennedy's stirring words from a month earlier in Houston, when he declared, in a phrase of ringing rhetoric that still moves me deeply, America's ambition to land on the moon: "We choose to go to the moon. We choose to go to the moon in this decade and do the other things, not because they are easy but because they are hard, because that goal will serve to organize and measure the best of our energies and our skills." I listened then, and read these words today, and after more than forty years the inspiration has not dimmed.

But mostly, as the son of artists, I remember his conviction that the arts are a way in to the best of what the human animal has to offer. He had campaigned from a platform that stated plainly that a government is good that allows for free and full expression. "There is a connection, hard to explain logically but easy to feel," Kennedy said, "between achievement in public life and progress in the arts. The age of Pericles was also the age of Phidias. The age of Lorenzo de Medici was also the age of Leonardo da Vinci. The age of Elizabeth also the age of Shakespeare. And the New Frontier for which I campaign can also be a New Frontier for American art."

After he had achieved the presidency, Kennedy continued to speak out on behalf of art and artists. "The life of the arts," he said, "far from being an interruption or distraction in the life of a nation, is very close to the center of a nation's purpose—and it is the test of the quality of a nation's civilization."

On the evening of Monday, November 13, 1961, President Kennedy opened the doors of the White House East Room to a concert of chamber music featuring the celebrated cellist and political exile Pablo Casals. The eighty-four-year-old musician, who had protested the regime of Generalissimo Francisco Franco by leaving his native Spain for good decades before, was one of the signal artists and most principled figures of the twentieth century.

President Kennedy stood to inform the audience that Maestro Casals had first performed in that room at a reception given by President William McKinley in 1898, and that he had most recently played there in 1904 for President Theodore Roosevelt. And what an audience was there that night in 1961! Most of the country's greatest musicians had been invited, including conductors Leonard Bernstein, Eugene Ormandy, and Leopold Stokowski, and composers Samuel Barber, Elliott Carter, Aaron Copland, Henry Cowell, Howard Hanson, Roy Harris, Alan Hovhaness, Gian Carlo Menotti, Walter Piston, William Schuman, Roger Sessions, and Virgil Thomson. It may have been the most luminous gathering of American classical musicians in history.

For more than an hour, Casals and his fellow performers—violinist Alexander Schneider and pianist Mieczyslaw Horszowski—played music by Felix Mendelssohn, Robert Schumann, and François Couperin, and a Catalan folk song that Casals himself had arranged for cello and piano. After the concert there was dinner and dancing. A few weeks later Leonard Bernstein recalled that "Roy Harris and Walter Piston and people like that were kicking up their heels, a little high, just so delighted to be there, so glad that they had been asked, feeling that they had finally been recognized as honored artists of the Republic. You know, I've never seen so many happy artists in my life."

Maybe it wasn't Camelot, but for artists it might have been Valhalla.

On October 27, 1963, President Kennedy spoke at Amherst College in western Massachusetts in praise of the American poet Robert Frost. He had been eighty-six years old, with windblown white hair, his small rugged frame bundled against the bright January cold, when he had recited his poem "The Gift Outright" at Kennedy's inauguration in 1961. Robert Frost died two years later, and as late October brought its blazing colors to the Berkshires, Kennedy spoke of the poet's contributions to America and of all poets' contributions to the world.

> Robert Frost was one of the granite figures of our time. In America our heroes have customarily run to men of large accomplishments. But today this college and this country honor a man whose contribution was not to our size but to our spirit; not to our political beliefs but to our insight; not to our self-esteem but to our self-comprehension. In honoring Robert Frost, we therefore can pay honor to the deepest sources of our national strength. His poetry reminds us of the richness and diversity of human existence.
>
> For art establishes the basic human truths which must serve as the touchstones of our judgment. The artist, however faithful to his personal vision of reality, becomes the last champion of the individual mind and sensibility against an intrusive society and an officious state. The great artist is thus a solitary figure. He has, as Frost said, "a lover's quarrel with the world." In pursuing his perceptions of reality, he

must often sail against the currents of his time. This is not a popular role.

I look forward to a great future for America—a future in which our country will match its military strength with our moral restraint, its wealth with our wisdom, its power with our purpose. I look forward to an America which will not be afraid of grace and beauty. And I look forward to an America which commands respect throughout the world not only for its strength but for its civilization as well.

Less than a month after uttering those words, President Kennedy went to Dallas. America had been so inspired, so hopeful, so confident. The country was young again, we were moving forward, we had been challenged to lift spirits around the world and to raise our sights to the heavens. Perhaps all that promise had been an illusion, but in an instant that autumn our hope turned to fear, and soon thereafter would follow cynicism, insecurity, and dread. Youth and buoyant wit had been slain, and our leaders were suddenly old and gray again.

Like all of us who were alive and sentient at the time, my memories of Friday, November 22, 1963, are crystal clear and bordered in black. I was, as usual, attending Mrs.Snowberger's sixth-grade class at Lindbergh North Junior High School in St Louis, Missouri. At about twelve forty-five, our class had just returned from lunch, and Mrs. Snowberger, a shortish white-haired woman with a grandmotherly demeanor, was reviewing our recently completed leaf collection assignment. I had spent afternoons that autumn picking up leaves from oaks and elms, maples and chestnuts, willows and crabapples, and even a rare ginkgo that grew in the city's famous Forest Park, and pressing them between sheets of clear plastic. I was proud of my leaf collection and, from my desk in the fourth row, was impatiently waiting for Mrs. Snowberger to hold me up as an example for the rest of the class to emulate if they ever wanted to achieve anything in the highly competitive forestry industry.

But then we weren't talking about fallen leaves anymore. Without warning, the school's public address system crackled to life, and we found ourselves trying to understand what turned out to be the audio of a television news broadcast. For at least a minute we listened uncomprehendingly to an announcer reading details of a bulletin concerning a disruption of something called a motorcade in Dallas, Texas. And then we grasped the enormous truth that the president had been shot.

My chin cupped in my right palm, I turned my head to the right, my widened eyes meeting those of my friend Bill. "This is just like Lincoln," I said.

At one o'clock we filed off to gym class, but everyone just sat around on wrestling mats, nervously chattering in hushed voices. Then around one forty-five the school principal addressed us all, telling us that the president was dead and that we would be sent home immediately.

It was a rainy Friday in St. Louis. That evening my mother had no desire to cook, so we drove to a local shopping center where we'd seen Kennedy speak three years before. We ate dinner at a cafeteria and my father purchased, for seven cents at the Walgreen's drugstore, an Extra edition of the *St. Louis Post-Dispatch*. The headline, from the yellowing pages I have kept to this day, reads KENNEDY IS ASSASSINATED. SHOT BY SNIPER IN DALLAS.

We were all numb that weekend. Everything seemed to be happening in slow motion, even the unbelievable second murder, captured live on television Sunday morning, when strip club owner Jack Ruby stuck his gun into the ribs of accused assassin Lee Harvey Oswald and pulled the trigger. On Saturday evening, CBS televised a memorial concert to the dead president. Eugene Ormandy conducted the Philadelphia Orchestra. On Sunday evening, ABC televised a tribute to Kennedy that included Marian Anderson singing Negro spirituals and the actor Charlton Heston reading from the poetry of Robert Frost.

Monday, November 25, the day President Kennedy was buried, was declared a National Day of Mourning by the new President Johnson. Three things stand out in my memory of that solemn day. It saw the birth of my sense of moral outrage, as my friend Darryl chose to go hunting with his father on that holiday from school. I could not have been more certain of anything than I was that shooting innocent animals had no place on such a day. Secondly, I remember vividly the rhythm of the twenty-four drummers, their instruments muffled and draped in black cloth, as they accompanied the caisson on its deliberate, agonizing journey through the streets of Washington on its way to Arlington National Cemetery. The drummers kept up their ponderous and stately Dead March for what seemed like hours, the triple rhythm seemingly becoming synchronized with my own heavy heartbeat: one, two, three/one-two-three/one, two, three/one-two-three/one, two, three/one-two-three/one, two, and three. And over and over and over again.

Finally, I remember that National Day of Mourning as the only time I ever saw my mother cry. We were a family acquainted with grief, as my parents' families' lives had ended in Auschwitz, Riga, Terezin, and Trawniki. Yet we never spoke of such things in our house, and it was not until President Kennedy's coffin was lowered into the ground in Arlington, a solitary bugler cracking a note as he blew "Taps," that my mother, Rosemary, wept. What floods of grief those tears must have hidden.

Across the nation my mother's tears were duplicated many times over as families gathered around their television sets to watch and mourn. And in my house, we mourned the loss of a champion of the arts, the loss of one who sensed that music, poetry, and painting bind us together and remind us profoundly of what it means to be human.

An ancient Persian saying declares that "the deeper that sorrow carves into your being, the more joy you can contain." The Beatles would have swept America, as they swept the world, had there been no assassination. But we were carved deeply in November 1963 and needed the joy of the Beatles' art to fill and heal the wound. The feelings of exhilaration and immortality that great art confers were so sorely needed after that brutal proof that life is transient.

The Beatles thus reminded us of another example of ancient wisdom: *Vita brevis, ars longa*.

The holiday season of 1963 seemed dreary, colder, and gloomier than usual. And then, as the country and the hemisphere lurched toward the darkest days of the year, a song was released on the day after Christmas. A hand was outstretched to us all.

It was, and remains, a great song, a joyous, reassuring sentiment riding gently atop an exuberantly beautiful melody. And it will always be Our Song, the song that, more than any other, introduced us Americans to the Beatles. I think it is safe to say that all of us who call upon our first memories of hearing the band on the radio think of December 1963 and January 1964 and hear, playing sweetly in our mind's ear, "I Want to Hold Your Hand."

"I remember when we got the chord that made that song," recalled John Lennon near the end of his life. "We were in Jane Asher's house, downstairs in the cellar, playing on the piano at the same time, and we had 'Oh, you-u-u . . . got that something . . .' And Paul hits this chord and I turn to him and say, 'That's it! Do that again!' In those days, we really used to absolutely write like that—both playing into each other's noses."

But the song is so much more than a single chord, of course. The words may be simple, but they express tender longing and the heartfelt magic of human touch in a sentiment both innocent and profoundly worldly. And the music—"It's beautiful, the kind of song I like to sing," said

John—underscores the meaning of the words with an artistry of which master melodist Franz Schubert would be proud.

The song opens with a series of five descending phrases:

1. Oh, yeah I'll (E down to B)
2. Tell you something (C up to D then down to A)
3. I think you'll understand (B down to F-sharp)
4. When I (again E down to B)
5. Say that something (again C to D down to A)

It's only then, after establishing that downward flowing line, that the melody leaps up an entire octave to land joyfully on the word "hand," the punchline of the song. The first lines are all breathless anticipation, and when the central idea of the lover's message is delivered, it comes bursting out in a manner that transcends everything that's come before. It's simple, direct, and utterly magical, the essence of lasting art.

There's a hush at the start of the bridge ("And when I touch you I feel happy inside") that leads to an exuberance made all the more explosive because of that hush: "It's such a feeling that my love I can't hide, I can't hide, I can't hide!" John's and Paul's voices achieve a gleeful and glorious harmony at the climax.

The end of the song offers new harmonic delights, as a brand-new chord is unveiled just before the title line is repeated for the last time and new vocal harmonies grace the final expression of "hold your hand." And as if all that were not enough, two sets of triplets broaden out the rhythm under the last word before the final cadence arrives. The very effort of stopping such a runaway train of emotion helps us realize what an exhilarating ride it has been.

Those triplets point to another, more subterranean reason that "I Want to Hold Your Hand" may have had such a profound effect on the American consciousness, or subconsciousness. A triple meter accompanies the emotional climax of the song, the (thrice) repeated ejaculations of the phrase "I can't hide." That same meter serves as the song's introduction, hammered out by John's and George's ringing guitars. Only a little more than a month before, another triple rhythm had been at the heavy heart of the Dead March played by the muffled drums that accompanied President Kennedy's caisson on its solemn march through the streets of Washington. I can still close my eyes and summon an image of the black-and-white telecast of the funeral, and the soundtrack of the broadcast is that slow and stately triple meter.

Rhythm is the strongest and most elemental connection we have to music. Is it possible that the joyful triple meter heard right at the outset, then again at the song's high point, and finally at the very end somehow registered with us as we struggled to throw off the gloom of November 1963, and we subconsciously heard "I Want to Hold Your Hand" not only as an offered gesture of love but also as a gentle reminder that life goes on after death? Did the song connect a painful past to a hopeful future? Were there extramusical forces at work?

In my hometown of St. Louis, my top-40 radio station of choice, KXOK, could have had a jump on its competitors. The afternoon drive-time DJ, Don "Stinky" Shaffer, received a phone call one day in the fall of 1963 from a woman with an English accent who identified herself as living in southern Illinois, well within the reach of KXOK's signal. She told Shaffer that she'd married an American GI and had come to live in America, but that her younger brother was back in England and a member of a very popular band. She offered to drive to St. Louis and play her brother's record for him. Shaffer warily agreed, and the next afternoon the woman arrived at the studio, bearing an advanced pressing of her brother's latest hit single, not yet even released in the United Kingdom. She played the record for Shaffer and KXOK's operations director Bud Cannell. Shaffer recalls thinking the record sounded like "country music with a British accent" and assured the woman that the record wouldn't work for the KXOK audience. So Louise Harrison Caldwell went home to Illinois and KXOK missed out on the chance to introduce her brother George's band's "I Want to Hold Your Hand" to America.

Within weeks, another American radio station would claim that honor, and the entire country would begin to experience "such a feeling."

8

"The Beatles Are Coming!"

Like an approaching thunderstorm, the Beatles' arrival in America was preceded by a few low rumbles and flashes of light, none of them giving more than the slightest hint of the potency to follow. Noting the saturation coverage in England of the Beatles' Royal Command Performance two weeks earlier, *Newsweek* magazine offered one of the first American impressions of the band and its music. The tone of condescension and contempt in an article in the issue of November 18, 1963, would set a standard that virtually all American media would follow for months.

"They wear sheep-dog bangs," began the article. "They are the Beatles, and the sound of their music is one of the most persistent noises heard over England since the air-raid sirens were dismantled. . . . Beatle music is high-pitched, loud beyond reason, and stupefyingly repetitive. Like rock 'n' roll, to which it is closely allied, it is even more effective to watch than to hear. They prance, skip, and turn in circles; Beatles have even been known to kiss their guitars." The uncredited author of the piece quoted a Beatle fan exclaiming, "Oh dearie me, they just send the joy out to you," but apparently caught none of the joy himself.

On November 21, the *CBS Evening News* aired a three-minute report about the Beatles. Much of the tape had been gathered during a performance of "She Loves You" at the Winter Gardens in Bournemouth on the sixteenth. The reporter, Alexander Kendrick, was also dismissive, referring to the Beatles as "merely the latest objects of adolescent adulation and culturally the modern manifestation of compulsive tribal singing and dancing." He concluded, "They symbolize the 20th century non-hero as they make non-music, wear non-haircuts, give no 'Mersey.' Meanwhile, yeah, yeah, yeah, the fan mail keeps rolling in and so does the money."

The news the next day, and indeed for the following several weeks, was dominated by the tragedy in Dallas. But on Tuesday, December 10, the *CBS Evening News* ran a slightly reedited version of its November 21 story on the Beatles. Watching in suburban Washington, D.C., was a fifteen-year-old junior high school student named Marsha Albert. Ignoring the manner in which she was being talked down to by correspondent Kendrick, Marsha was intrigued to learn of this band that had already won the hearts of English schoolgirls. Taking a cue from Chuck Berry's "Roll Over Beethoven," she wrote a little letter and sent it to her local DJ. In this case it was the man known in Washington as "CJ the DJ," Carroll James of radio station WWDC. Her letter asked James to play the newest song by the Beatles.

Befuddled at first by Marsha's request, James asked a staffer at the station, Jo Wilson, how he should go about finding a recording. Jo had a friend who worked as a flight attendant for the British airline BOAC; a phone call to London sent the stewardess to a record shop for a copy of the hot-selling single, and she brought it with her on her next flight to Washington. When the record arrived at WWDC, James called Marsha and asked her to come down to the studio to help him introduce it. At 5:15 P.M. on Tuesday the seventeenth, reading from a script that CJ the DJ had written for her, Marsha Albert announced, "Ladies and gentlemen, for the first time in America, here are the Beatles singing 'I Want to Hold Your Hand.'"

The reaction from WWDC's listeners was immediate and overwhelmingly positive—not a sure thing, as WWDC was a decidedly MOR, or middle of the road, station, with a playlist that tended toward the easy-listening end of the musical spectrum. Andy Williams, Al Hirt, Bobby Vinton, Steve Lawrence and Eydie Gorme, and Ruby and the Romantics were what WWDC listeners expected to hear on an early winter evening, and "I Want to Hold Your Hand" must have been something of a shock. But the shock was pure electricity, and in response Carroll James began playing the song over and over, fading it down in the middle to announce "This is a Carroll James exclusive" to prevent other stations from recording it and offering it as their own.

But other stations soon obtained copies in other ways,

and their broadcasts, following in the pioneering footsteps of WWDC, resulted in a major change of plans for Capitol Records. Dave Dexter, still the man in charge at Capitol, had once again astounded George Martin and Brian Epstein by insisting that he knew America better than they did, confidently predicting that "I Want to Hold Your Hand" would not sell in the States. This time, however, Epstein decided that he would not take no for an answer. Going over Dexter's head, he managed to secure the ears of Alan Livingston, the president of Capitol Records. Drawing upon the full range of his acting experience and insisting sincerely that the new single had been specifically produced with the American market in mind, Epstein per- suaded Livingston to release "I Want to Hold Your Hand" on his label. Rather than use the English B side, "This Boy," Livingston decided to reconfigure the single by put- ting "I Saw Her Standing There" on the flip side, thus beginning several years of confusion during which American pressings of Beatles singles and albums differed significantly from their English counterparts.

The plan was to release the new single in America in mid-January, but thanks to Marsha Albert and Carroll James, Capitol had to switch gears in a hurry. In the week before Christmas, demand for "I Want to Hold Your Hand" became unrelenting. Suddenly Vee-Jay and Swan, the two little labels that had stepped into the breach cre- ated by Capitol, decided to capitalize on the frenzy by reis- suing their older singles and claiming that they were the true home of the Beatles. Capitol reacted swiftly and ruth- lessly, filing cease-and-desist lawsuits against Vee-Jay and

Swan, reacquiring the rights to the Beatle songs it had earlier passed on, and moving up its own release date for the new single to the day after Christmas. Meanwhile, events had been set in motion that would transport the band across the ocean and its fans to unheard-of peaks of joy and excitement.

Everyone, understandably, wants to be first, and also to be credited with being first. Most Americans, especially those of us who watch TV, think of Ed Sullivan as the man who brought the Beatles to America. But that title rightly belongs to Sid Bernstein.

In the spring of 1963, Bernstein was forty-four years old. The adopted son of Russian immigrants, he had worked in his father's tailor shop before developing an interest in promoting and presenting musicians. Throughout the 1950s, Bernstein produced shows at such New York City venues as the Paramount and Apollo theaters and the Newport Jazz Festival in Rhode Island. He produced the comeback tour of Judy Garland and booked Tony Bennett for a career-altering concert at Carnegie Hall. As an agent for New York's General Artists Corporation, Bernstein worked with such jazz and blues musicians as Miles Davis, Muddy Waters, Ray Charles, and Fats Domino. So it came naturally to him to keep an eye out for new opportunities, and when he began reading excited accounts in English newspapers about a hot new band from Liverpool, he decided that he had to have them.

Through a fortuitous encounter with a man who was trying to promote the Beatles for Vee-Jay Records,

Bernstein acquired the phone number of Brian Epstein's home in London. At first, Epstein resisted the idea of coming to America. No English popular music star had ever succeeded in the States, and Epstein was insistent that his boys should never again have to play to an empty house. Why would he want to commit professional suicide by taking an unknown band over there, Epstein wanted to know. But Bernstein, acting on a hunch that the Beatles would translate to America, impulsively offered $6,500 for two concerts on a single day at Carnegie Hall, not even knowing at that moment if the owners of the hall would be amenable.

When Epstein showed interest, the two began to discuss dates. Bernstein was all for having the show occur later in 1963, but Epstein cautiously insisted on waiting until the Beatles began to get greater airplay on American radio. So Bernstein suggested February 12, 1964; it was Lincoln's Birthday, he pointed out, and kids would be off from school. Epstein agreed, and the deal was done.

This is probably the place to demolish at least one myth about the Beatles. They had already demonstrated their musical integrity in countless ways, but after their visit to America they attempted to forge another tale of their indomitable belief in themselves by saying that they had refused to cross the Atlantic until one of their songs had made it to number one on the American charts. Once "I Want to Hold Your Hand" had made it to that lofty position, they pointed out proudly, they felt the time was now right and a deal to travel Stateside could be pursued. But Sid Bernstein's agreement with Brian Epstein was achieved months before that great song was even recorded, much less released in America. The Beatles were now committed to an American performance, come what may.

Epstein, however, was not the sort of man who would leave things to chance. Days after the Beatles' immense success at the Royal Command Performance, he flew to New York to help prepare the ground for the Carnegie Hall date and to spread the word about the Beatles even further afield via the American media. To secure expanded radio coverage, he planned to meet with executives of Capitol Records. And, convinced of the power of television by the phenomenal nationwide response to the Beatles' appearances on both the London Palladium and Command Performance broadcasts, Epstein was determined to showcase his boys on American television. For that he would have to meet Mr. Ed Sullivan.

In November 1963, Ed Sullivan had been the ruler of Sunday night TV for the better part of fifteen years, ever since the night of June 20, 1948, when, as the host of a program called *Toast of the Town*, he had first ambled out onstage in front of the cameras of the Columbia Broadcasting System. Born in 1901 of Irish parentage, Sullivan had worked in radio and motion pictures and had achieved a moderate success as a show-biz columnist for the *New York Daily News*, though his readership never approached the numbers enjoyed by his rival wordsmith Walter Winchell. Thanks to the infancy and innocence of the brave new medium in 1948, Sullivan's awkwardness and wooden delivery (the stuff of countless impressionists) were not seen as drawbacks by the CBS brass, and almost from the start Sullivan's earnest introductions of his wide-ranging acts were enthusiastically embraced by Sunday-night audiences.

The very haphazardness of the show's vaudevillian bill of fare was a major part of its charm and appeal. Such "serious" stars as Maria Callas, Rudolf Nureyev, and Charles Laughton shared the spotlight with comics and dog acts, tumblers and gymnasts, prizewinning Iowa steers, the quiz show superstar Charles Van Doren, and the man who skipped nimbly across the stage as he kept dinner plates twirling on the top of long, slender sticks. On September 9, 1955, after first turning down the chance and being scooped by Steve Allen, Ed Sullivan had presented one of the Beatles' heroes, Elvis Presley. Brian Epstein knew that the Sullivan show was the perfect venue to introduce the Beatles to America and hoped to secure a spot for them. What he didn't know was that Ed Sullivan wanted to make a deal as well, thanks to a contact Epstein had already made.

Peter Prichard was an agent for the British show business moguls Lew and Leslie Grade and was also the major European talent coordinator for Ed Sullivan. It was through Prichard's efforts that Sullivan regularly featured the sweet, squeaky-voiced Italian mouse Topo Gigio ("Kiss-a me good night, Eddie"). Prichard also secured an on-site coup for Sullivan by filming a performance of the Singing Nun at her convent in Belgium. Born Jeanine Deckers and serving at a Dominican convent under the name Sister Luc-Gabrielle, the Singing Nun won a

Grammy in 1963 for "Dominique," her light-hearted tribute to St. Dominic, the founder of her order. "Dominique"
enjoyed the number-one position on the *Billboard* chart
for four weeks in December 1963, and at the time securing
a taped performance of the song was yet another triumph
for the Sullivan show.

Peter Prichard was with Ed Sullivan when they witnessed a frenzied airport reception for the Beatles that
piqued the showman's interest. Most accounts report that
the date was October 31, 1963, when the band returned
from Sweden, but Prichard insists that the fateful airport
encounter occured several weeks earlier. In any event,
Sullivan instructed Prichard to keep his eyes on the Beatles
and to let him know when the time was right to book
them.

Through his association with the Grades, Peter Prichard
also knew Brian Epstein. Lew Grade had produced *Sunday
Night at the Palladium,* and during preparations for the
Beatles' appearance at the Palladium on October 13, the
agent and manager became friendly. When Prichard
learned of Epstein's plans to fly to New York to secure a
place on American television, Prichard told him, "Don't
see anyone else before you see Ed Sullivan." On Tuesday,
November 5, the morning after the Royal Command
Performance, Prichard gathered together all of the rapturous reviews from the night before and sent them via a
TWA flight attendant to Ed Sullivan's attention. He also
put in a transatlantic telephone call to Sullivan to tell him
the time to book the Beatles had come. So when Epstein,
Sullivan, and Sullivan's producer and son-in-law, Bob

Precht, met in Sullivan's office at the Delmonico Hotel on November 11, everyone was inclined to make a deal.

Since Sid Bernstein had already secured Carnegie Hall for Wednesday, February 12, it made sense to consider either the previous or the following Sunday for the TV broadcast. Shrewdly, Sullivan chose both; he offered Epstein slots on the program of February 9, to be broadcast from the CBS studios in Manhattan, and the program of February 16, scheduled to air live from the Deauville Hotel in Miami. In addition, Epstein agreed that the Beatles would tape some performances for Sullivan's show of February 23. The band would be paid scale, or $3,500, for each appearance, plus airfare.

It was a good deal for both sides. Sullivan secured the live American debut of a band he assumed would become a major attraction, and he got the rights cheaply. Epstein, knowing full well the poor rate of success of previous English stars in America, was at least assured of giving his boys the best of all possible stages for their debut.

With the broadcast and stage appearances worked out, plus an additional performance scheduled for February 11 in Washington (home of Marsha Albert and Carroll James), it was time for Capitol Records to throw its full weight behind the Beatles' American bow. Alan Livingston agreed to spend $50,000 on a massive public relations blitz organized around the message "The Beatles Are Coming!" Capitol Records printed five million stickers with that slogan and managed to affix nearly all of them to trees, telephone poles, and mailboxes throughout the country. Receptionists at the Capitol offices were instructed to answer the telephone by saying, "Hello, Capitol Records—the Beatles are coming!" Capitol printed buttons that read "Be a Beatles Booster" and sent them to radio stations and record shops. They arranged for a Beverly Hills hairstylist named Gene Shacove to create an imitation Beatle cut and sent out photographs of Neile Adams (Mrs. Steve McQueen) modeling the new 'do. Not satisfied with a real hairstyle, they mailed officially sanctioned Beatle wigs to local distributors and encouraged their sale to record buyers. They even tried, but failed, to get University of Wisconsin cheerleaders to display "The Beatles Are Coming!" placards during the Rose Bowl on January 1, 1964. And, despite the winter season, a new ice cream flavor, Beatlenut, was introduced. Most importantly, Capitol Records set its record-pressing plants to their highest states of alertness, mandating twenty-four-hour shifts in order to meet the demand for copies of "I Want to Hold Your Hand" and their first Beatles album. The single came out on December 26, considerably brightening the holiday season, and by January 10 it had already sold a million copies. The album, called *Meet the Beatles* and featuring the same Robert Freeman photograph as the English *With the Beatles* (but with only twelve songs to the English album's fourteen), was issued on January 20. In its first week, it sold four hundred thousand copies.

Beatlemania had finally overcome America. No major newspaper, magazine, or television or radio station was without its story on the Beatles or, more accurately, on the Beatles phenomenon. Sales figures formed the core of each story, as did cute details about the wigs and fan clubs that editors apparently found irresistible. American radio stations had finally caught on, and the Beatles' singles were all over the airwaves. It must have been otherwise, but all I remember of late December 1963 and the first weeks of 1964 is Johnny Rabbit and Stinky Shaffer introducing "She Loves You" and "I Want to Hold Your Hand" over and over again on KXOK. The Beatles were the newest fad, the latest hula hoop or Davy Crockett coonskin cap to be embraced by an eager American public. In the midst of all the hype and hoopla, it was probably inevitable that the core of the Beatles' appeal, their music, would be overshadowed by the ephemera.

But as 1963 came to a close, William Mann, the chief classical music critic of the *London Times,* published an extraordinary appreciation of the Beatles as musicians, a reminder to all who cared to listen of what all the fuss was really about. Headlined "What Songs the Beatles Sang," Mann's article began by stating, "The outstanding English composers of 1963 must seem to have been John Lennon and Paul McCartney, the talented young musicians from Liverpool whose songs have been sweeping the country since last Christmas." He went on to declare firmly that all the Beatles balloons and handbags, the screaming at Beatles concerts, everything he called the "social phenomenon of Beatlemania," interested him not at all; it was the music that mattered.

Mann pointed out that English popular music had taken its cues from America for decades and that the inventive, imaginative, and decidedly English character of the

Beatles was both welcome and the source of "a nice flattering irony" now that the band was becoming an American favorite as well. He recognized the importance of the fact that three of the Beatles composed their own songs and yet credited them with presenting other musicians' material in a manner that was both faithful to the original and yet wonderfully consistent with their own style. Without a trace of condescension or irony, Mann compared aspects of Beatles harmonies favorably with those of classical composers Gustav Mahler and Peter Maxwell Davies. And he listed a number of aspects of the band's "trademark" musicality, ranging from their "exhilarating and often quasi-instrumental vocal duetting" to their translations of African and American musical idioms into a "tough, sensitive Merseyside" sound that was distinctive and utterly original.

William Mann concluded his insightful essay by declaring his continuing interest in what the Beatles would offer next and wondering "if America will spoil them or hold onto them." America, it turned out, would amaze them, and they us.

9

"A Vision of the Ecstasy of Life"

As a prelude to their journey to America, the Beatles flew east to France. On January 14, 1964, three days after "I Want to Hold Your Hand" entered the American *Cashbox* charts at number eighty, they took up residence in sumptuous quarters in the George V Hotel in Paris. For three weeks they performed at the Olympia Theater, topping a bill that also included Sylvie Vartan and Trini Lopez. Other than their regular employment at the Cavern in Liverpool and along the Reeperbahn in Hamburg, the Olympia was the Beatles' longest engagement of their career. John and Paul had a piano sent up to their suite, and they spent many hours writing six new songs for the forthcoming film *A Hard Day's Night*.

Paris also became the only city outside the United Kingdom where the Beatles made recordings when, later that month, they assembled, somewhat unwillingly, in the Pathé Marconi Studios to make a disc for what was still a huge German fan base. The German division of EMI had persuaded George Martin to convince the band to make a German-language version of their two biggest hits, "She Loves You" and "I Want to Hold Your Hand." With the assistance of a German language coach named Otto Demmlar, the Beatles produced "Sie Liebt Dich" and "Komm, Gibt Mir Deine Hand," which means "Come, give me your hand." It's a subtle, though important, difference in meaning, but in the end it didn't really matter; the original sold just as well in Germany as it did everywhere else in the world.

Late on the night of Friday, January 17, a representative of Capitol Records sent a telegram to Brian Epstein in Paris. Epstein immediately called George Martin and the Beatles to tell them the electrifying news: "I Want to Hold Your Hand" had reached number one on the *Cashbox* charts. "We couldn't believe it," remembers Ringo. "We all just started acting like people from Texas, hollering and shouting 'Ya-hoo!'" They gathered for a celebratory meal, and the ordinarily staid Brian Epstein wore a chamber pot on his head. None of them got to bed before dawn.

All seemed in perfect readiness for their trip to America. It was, as George Harrison observed dryly, "handy to have a number one" record as their journey began. But nothing was assured, and there was the unenviable precedent of previous English pop stars with which to contend. Cliff Richard and Adam Faith, two huge stars in England, had gone to America and, as John Lennon said, "died. . . . Cliff was fourteenth on the bill with Frankie Avalon." Ringo said to a Liverpool reporter, "They've got everything over there; will they want us, too?" The Beatles were so unsure of what might occur in America that, perhaps in a superstitious attempt to alter fate, they entered into a bet proposed by the American composer and record producer Quincy Jones, whom they met in Paris. Jones, joined by Brian and Paul, wagered one hundred dollars that the Beatles would be a success in the States; John, George, and Ringo took the opposite stance.

Had they known how close they'd come to not enjoying their televised springboard in America, they might all have bet against themselves. On his television show of January 3, Jack Paar showed an extended clip of a Beatles performance, infuriating his rival, Ed Sullivan, with whom he'd been carrying on an on-air feud. Sullivan immediately called Peter Prichard in England and demanded that he cancel the Beatles' contract to appear on his shows in February. "Pay them off and get rid of them," Sullivan growled. "Like a good agent," says Prichard, "I did nothing." A few days later, Sullivan called back to reverse himself, and a small crisis was averted.

On the morning of Friday, February 7, the journey began. Pan Am flight 101 left London's Heathrow Airport bearing the four Beatles, John's wife, Cynthia, Brian Epstein, roadies Neil Aspinall and Mal Evans, publicist Brian Sommerville, American record producer Phil Spector, one of Spector's girl groups, the Ronettes (one of whom George Harrison had been dating), assorted businessmen hoping to catch Epstein's ear, and photographer Harry Benson. Benson, a native of Glasgow, had begun his career snapping photos of vacationers at Butlins Holiday

Camp, the same venue where Ringo had played with Rory Storm, but more recently he had established a solid reputation as a photojournalist, reporting from independence rallies in Africa and freedom rides in the American South. His paper, London's *Daily Express,* had assigned him to cover the Beatles in Paris and then extended the assignment by sending him to New York.

During much of the seven-hour flight, Benson remembers, the Beatles paced nervously about, trying to overcome their emotions by talking and laughing. At the same time, New York radio stations WINS, WMCA, and WABC provided their listeners with constant updates on the plane's progress ("It's 6:30 A.M. on B-Day! The Beatles left London thirty minutes ago, headed for New York!"), counting down the hours and then the minutes until touchdown. Murray Kaufman, the DJ who called himself Murray the K, led the charge for WINS, while one of its rivals started referring to itself as WA-Beatles-C. Thanks in part to the stations' promotions, a crowd of young people began to gather at John F. Kennedy Airport.

Reports of the throng were passed to the Pan Am pilot, who relayed the news back to the Beatles. But when the plane touched down at JFK at one-twenty that afternoon, no one on board was prepared for the size of the crowd that clung to the roof of the International Arrivals Building. Estimates ranged from three thousand to ten thousand people. Signs sprouted everywhere, mostly welcoming the band but with a few exceptions, such as "Beatles Unfair to Bald Men" and "England Get Out of

Ireland!" When the Beatles emerged from the plane and walked down the gangway, waving and smiling, a persistent high-pitched shriek escaped the throats of the thousands, competing with the wails of jet engines for sonic supremacy. A front-page story in the next day's *New York Times*, headlined "The Beatles Invade, Complete with Long Hair and Screaming Fans," quoted an airport official as saying, "We've never seen anything like this here before. Never. Not even for kings and queens." The Beatles were impressed and hugely relieved. But demonstrating that he was also aware of issues far from the world of pop music, John turned to Harry Benson and asked, "Where are all the Freedom Riders?"

Hustled through customs and away from crowds of girls who wept and beat balled fists against their heads in an agony of desire for closer contact, the Beatles were met by more than two hundred writers, photographers, and radio and television correspondents. Thanks in part to President Kennedy's deft handling of such affairs, press conferences had become a popular way for the media and the public to size up a subject. The Beatles' performance in the Pan Am lounge, as they parried the reporters' frequently dismissive and ludicrous questions, provided America with a first glimpse of their sharp and biting wit.

Reporter: "Will you sing for us?"
John: "We need money first."
Reporter: "How many of you are bald so you have to wear those wigs?"

Beatles, in unison: "Oh, we're all bald."

John: "And I'm deaf and dumb."

Reporter: "Are you for real? And are you going to get a haircut?"

George: "I had one yesterday."

Reporter: "What do you think about the campaign in Detroit to stamp out the Beatles?"

Paul: "We've got a campaign to stamp out Detroit."

Reporter: "Are you part of a social rebellion against the older generation?"

John: "It's a dirty lie!"

Reporter: "What is your ambition?"

Paul: "To come to America."

Reporter: "What do you do in your hotel rooms between concerts?"

George: "Ice skate."

Reporter: "Why does your music excite your fans so much?"

John: "If we knew that, we'd form another group and be managers."

Reporter: "What do you think of America?"

Ringo: "They all seem out of their minds."

That press conference, and a photo shoot in Central Park on Saturday, helped establish the Beatles' reputations as clever and endearing. John later looked back on such encounters with a mixture of bemusement and frustration. What struck the journalists as so witty, he said, was just schoolboy humor, tossed off by the Beatles because of the inanity of most of the questions. Had anyone asked a serious question about their music, John said, they would have answered seriously. But they never were given the opportunity and instead settled for what they considered a less worthy reputation as comedians.

After meeting the press, the Beatles rode into the city in black Cadillac limousines. Paul, sitting with John and Ringo, carried a transistor radio and exulted when hearing the blanket coverage the Beatles were getting from seemingly every New York radio station. When the limo reached Manhattan and stopped at a traffic light, the car was immediately surrounded by young fans who, once they saw that three real live Beatles were sitting inside, began pounding on the windows and screaming with excitement. The limo was then rescued by a contingent of mounted police, and the boys were escorted the rest of the way to their destination at the Plaza Hotel by a herd of galloping horses. Such forceful images did much to further the impression that the Beatles were, indeed, invading America.

The scene at the Plaza was no less chaotic and exciting than the airport arrival had been. Tom Wolfe, who was on the cusp of unveiling what would soon be known as the New Journalism, described the atmosphere in a front-page story for the next day's *New York Herald Tribune:*

At the Plaza Hotel there were police everywhere. The Plaza, on Central Park South just off Fifth Avenue, is one of the most sedate hotels in New York. The Plaza was petrified. The Plaza accepted the Beatles' reservations months ago, before knowing it was a rock-and-roll group that attracts teenage riots.

About 500 teenagers, most of them girls, had shown up at the Plaza. The police had herded most of them behind barricades in the square between the hotel and the avenue. Every entrance to the hotel was guarded. The screams started as soon as the first limousine came into view.

The Beatles jumped out fast at the Fifth Avenue entrance. The teenagers had all been kept at bay. Old ladies ran up and touched the Beatles on their arms and backs as they ran up the stairs. The kids were still hanging around the Plaza hours after they went inside.

One group of girls asked everybody who came out, "Did you see the Beatles? Did you touch them?" A policeman came up, and one of them yelled, "He touched a Beatle! I saw him!" The girls jumped on the cop's arms and back, but it wasn't a mob assault. There were goony smiles all over their faces.

Inside the Plaza, the Beatles spread out over a ten-room suite on the twelfth floor. They continued to be amazed and very happy with their reception, listening to their songs played over and over on New York radio stations, calling in requests (for songs by Marvin Gaye, Chuck Berry, and the Shirelles, not their own), and joshing on air with Murray the K on WINS. They watched the evening news on CBS and saw Walter Cronkite narrate their tumultuous arrival.

That evening they received a representative from *The Ed Sullivan Show*, production secretary Emily Cole, who came

to secure the lyrics for the songs the Beatles would perform on Sunday night. Everything that was to be spoken
or sung had to appear in the show's master script, which
would determine which camera would be used for each
shot. So Emily and John spent about thirty minutes
together, he dictating the words from the songs and she
dutifully taking them down. She remembers him as very
cordial and polite.

The tumult outside the hotel continued as hundreds of
kids maintained their vigil, many of them dressed in
Beatles sweatshirts and clutching copies of *Meet the Beatles,*
the band's first American album. A silent vigil it certainly
was not; every few minutes, the crowd launched into a
Beatles song, or they began singing a variation on the ditty
from the Broadway show *Bye Bye Birdie* ("We love you
Conrad, oh yes we do!" with the word "Conrad," as in
Conrad Birdie, changed to "Beatles"), or they simply
began chanting, "We want the Beatles!" over and over.
Hope sprang eternal that one of the Beatles would come
down or at least peer out a window.

That night, George Harrison began feeling the effects of
the long flight, the cold weather, and general fatigue. By
Saturday morning, he was suffering flulike symptoms and a
sore throat. (The *New York Times* quoted a policeman,
commenting sarcastically on the vocal skills of the Beatles,
asking, "How do they know he's got a sore throat?") His
sister, Louise, was summoned from her home in Illinois to
care for him, and he remained in bed while the other three
slipped out a side door and entertained reporters and
photographers at the Boat House in Central Park, again

charming everyone. From there they traveled to the old Hammerstein Theater at Broadway and 53rd Street, the site of CBS-TV's Studio 50 where, the following night, they would headline *The Ed Sullivan Show*. Roadie Neil Aspinall stood in for George at the sound check. Members of the Sullivan show's production staff were surprised when the Beatles asked to hear the results of the sound check; most of the bands who had appeared on the show had shown no interest in such details.

Bill Bohnert was the show's production designer and John Moffitt the associate director. Today they, along with Emily Cole Meisler, recall that much of that week leading up to the Sunday night broadcast felt very normal. There was the usual production meeting on Tuesday, February 4, presided over by producer Bob Precht. Nothing was said of that week's headline act or of the unprecedented demand for tickets. The studio held 728 seats and more than fifty thousand requests had been tallied, but they had all been handled by people in the CBS offices, far away from the production staff. At the end of the week, asked his opinion of the Beatles' appeal and his assessment of their staying power, Ed Sullivan's music director, Ray Block, declared, "The only thing that's different is the hair, as far as I can see. I give them a year." "Nobody," says John Moffitt today, "realized the impact to come, how momentous it would be."

On Sunday, February 9, crowds began to gather outside the theater by nine-thirty in the morning. Fifty-two police officers and ten mounted police did their best to keep a semblance of order. The throng was large, enthusiastic, and good-humored. Radio station WMCA, one of the leading outlets of Beatles cheerleading, had distributed yellow sweatshirts that pictured the staff DJs and the slogan "WMCA Good Guys." In response, a listener to one of New York's classical music stations had devised his own sweatshirt sporting the words "WQXR Bad Guys" and displayed it at the corner of 53rd and Broadway to light-hearted taunts.

Early that afternoon the Beatles took part in the dress rehearsal for the evening's live telecast and recorded three songs for the Sullivan show that would air on February 23. Disdaining the details of the program, Ed Sullivan always waited until the dress rehearsal to make his initial appearance and issue some final directives. This particular Sunday there was a huge crush of photographers, all eagerly crawling over each other like ants, to snap the Beatles. Bob Precht gave the photographers thirty minutes to shoot while the band stood around good-naturedly. Walter Cronkite's two teenage daughters, Nancy and Kathy, were among the well connected who had secured tickets to the theater for that day. Nancy recalls that a photographer suggested that Paul give her a kiss for the cameras and he gallantly refused.

Production designer Bill Bohnert had created two sets for the evening's two appearances by the band. His favorite was a black backdrop with the word "Beatles" cut out of it. Through the use of colored lights shining on a scrim behind the set, the word could change colors and present what Bohnert thought of as a pretty dazzling effect. But because the presence of all the photographers gave Sullivan the opportunity to demonstrate who really ran the show, he told Bohnert, in front of everybody, "Everyone knows who the Beatles are—we won't use that set." So Bohnert had to settle for his second set, a series of arrows pointing toward the spot where the Beatles would perform. As it happens, thanks to the notoriety of the appearance, the arrow set became Bohnert's best-known creation.

As showtime approached, the excitement in the theater mounted with each passing minute. "The kids were going crazy," remembers John Moffitt. More than once, Ed Sullivan addressed the audience, reminding them that there were other acts scheduled for that evening and that he expected absolute courtesy. "If you don't keep quiet," he threatened humorously, "I'm going to send for a barber." Tensions were also rising backstage. With just a few minutes remaining, Brian Epstein walked up to Sullivan, who was scribbling notes on a clipboard. "I would like to know the exact wording of your introduction," he said imperiously. Sullivan didn't even look up. "I would like *you* to get lost," he growled.

The Ed Sullivan Show was the only network program to begin at eight o'clock on Sunday evening in February 1964, and of course at the time there were only three networks. NBC's one-hour *Walt Disney's Wonderful World of Color* aired at seven-thirty and that night presented the first of a three-part telling of "The Scarecrow of Romney Marsh," starring Secret Agent- and Prisoner-to-be Patrick McGoohan. ABC offered a one-hour family Western series, also starting at seven-thirty, called *The Travels of Jaimie McPheeters,* featuring Dan O'Herlihy. Ray Walston and Bill Bixby starred in the hit CBS sitcom *My Favorite Martian,* which began at seven-thirty and was the lead-in for Sullivan.

At nine o'clock, CBS presented another high-powered hour of television as Judy Garland performed a solo concert on her weekly musical variety program. NBC presented its hit Western series *Bonanza,* with Lorne Greene and the Cartwright family bringing law and order to Virginia City. But how many of us remember watching any of those programs that night? At eight o'clock, when the black-and-white picture on our screens showed a curtain going up on *The Ed Sullivan Show,* as it did each week, how could we have imagined how apt that image was? Something very important began for us that night.

A great roar went up from the studio audience when Ringo's Ludwig drum set was wheeled into position. Announcer Ralph Renick listed the sponsors for that night's show, including Anacin and Pillsbury, and then intoned, "And now here he is, Ed Sullivan!" With his distinctive nervous shuffle, Sullivan strolled into his position stage right and immediately announced that the Beatles (a word he insisted on pronouncing *Beat*-ulls) had just received a telegram from Elvis Presley and Colonel Tom Parker wishing them success in America. Sullivan then listed a number of big acts that had made their way across "our stage," including Topo Gigio, the Singing Nun, Milton Berle, Van Heflin, "and last Sunday, the never-to-be-forgotten teaming of Sammy Davis Jr. and Ella Fitzgerald." Now, he continued, "the whole country is waiting to hear England's Beatles . . . and you're going to hear them after this commercial!" Groans rose from the theater's seats as the screen cut to an ad for Aero Shave ("Keeps drenching your beard while others dry out!") and another for Griffin Liquid Shoe Polish.

When Sullivan returned to the screen he wore a mischievous grin, as though he knew that the tease had gone on long enough. Bobbing and weaving woodenly, his body seemingly controlled by strings worked in the wings above his head, he said, "Yesterday and today our theater has been jammed with reporters and photographers from all over the nation, and these veterans agree with me that the city has never witnessed the excitement stirred by these youngsters from Liverpool who call themselves the Beatles. Now tonight you're gonna twice be entertained by them, right now and again during the second half of our show. Ladies and gentlemen . . ." And Sullivan paused for a moment, relishing the anticipation.

". . . THE BEATLES, let's bring them out . . . " His right index finger led his body in a full whirl to his left as the showman directed our attention to something unseen but wonderful just out of view. What we at home saw first was not the Beatles but a shot of the studio audience. Smack in the middle of the camera's vision was a middle-aged man in horn-rimmed glasses. But he was surrounded by young people, mostly young girls, their faces aglow with joy and excitement, their mouths open, their eyes wide, their hands clapping or clasping each other or simply raised in supplication. Three years earlier, on a cold, snowy January day in Washington, the country had been told that "the torch has been passed to a new generation of Americans."

True as the president's words might have been on that day, here was visual evidence that the torch had been passed yet again, that a new generation was coming into existence before our eyes.

Slowly the image dissolved, and the shot of the joyful crowd mixed with, and then was replaced by, the Beatles themselves, occupying the center of Bill Bohnert's arrows. Whether or not it was director Tim Kiley's intention, those of us watching our televisions had experienced a direct identification between the audience, surrogates for all of us, and the musicians whom they, and we, had waited to see and hear. "I am he as you are he as you are me and we are all together," John Lennon would sing three years later, but we began to know that truth that February night.

The Beatles sang three songs in their first set, "All My Loving," "Till There Was You," and "She Loves You." The screen darkened to identify each member of the band in turn during "Till There Was You"; when John was ID'd, the screen read, "Sorry girls, he's married." John's microphone didn't seem to be working—his voice was nearly inaudible throughout the set—and the cameras concentrated on the other three, but during "She Loves You" there was an exquisite moment when John and George caught each other's eye and George positively beamed, an indication of their pleasure at how things were going.

Over the next forty minutes, *The Ed Sullivan Show* was its usual mix of vaudevillian excess. Magician Fred Kaps did a card trick in which the king of spades kept inserting itself into the action and a trick involving a seemingly bottomless salt shaker. Georgia Brown and the cast of *Oliver!*

offered a couple of songs from their hit show. Impressionist Frank Gorshin sent up Broderick Crawford, Dean Martin, Anthony Quinn, Marlon Brando, Burt Lancaster, Kirk Douglas, and Sir Alec Guinness in a matter of five minutes. Tessie O'Shea, a veteran of the British music hall, came out with an immense fur piece around her neck and a banjo in her hand to perform a medley of old songs. And the sketch team of McCall and Brill did an unfunny routine about the casting of a Hollywood movie.

Then Ed welcomed back the Beatles, and they sang "I Saw Her Standing There" and "I Want to Hold Your Hand." John's mike was still not functioning correctly, but the band rocked and they all looked very happy to be there. From time to time the cameras sought out members of the audience and revealed the joy, the fervor, the intox-ication that filled Studio 50. Girls were sometimes sitting quietly with expressions of awe on their young faces, some-times they clutched their heads and closed their eyes in bliss, occasionally they bounced up and down in their seats. They certainly screamed often enough, but never so loudly that they rendered the music inaudible. Most of the girls were in their teens, but during "I Want to Hold Your Hand" the camera found a woman who appeared to be at least thirty-five, and she was as ecstatic as anyone else. Everybody was just so damned happy, a pure emotion that, viewed forty years later, brings tears to my eyes.

Back then, of course, I was eleven and a half and com-pletely mystified by the girls' reactions. The next morning, as my friends and I rode to school on the bus, we spoke eagerly about the Beatles and wonderingly about the girls, slowly arriving at our first realization that girls were some-how *different*. So what made 'em scream, anyway?

Nancy Cronkite, fifteen at the time, planned to attend *The Ed Sullivan Show* in full makeup, including white lip-stick, to catch the attention of Ringo, her favorite Beatle. Her mother, however, made her remove it all before leav-ing the house. Today, Nancy says she screamed because of both excitement and peer pressure: "Your friends were screaming so you screamed, too."

But something else was afoot as well—something that would soon prove threatening to many Americans of both sexes: the emergence of a new female sexual identity and the birth of a second wave of feminism. The Beatles' much-mentioned long hair and high-heeled boots pro-vided hints of a feminine sensibility within the largely mas-culine world of rock 'n' roll. Professor Susan Douglas, in her book *Where the Girls Are,* points out that girls were drawn to the Beatles because they covered songs sung by "girl groups," because they were comfortable and had fun with their own image and identity, and because they were both sexy and reassuring. "They channeled sexual energy away from where Elvis had located it, in the male crotch," Douglas writes, "and moved it through safer, nonsexual parts of the body—their feet, their legs, their heads, their hair. Like electricity, it arced to the audience, where it surged safely through female limbs and faces. . . . For this, girls screamed in gratitude."

Douglas goes on to explain the almost universal expres-sions of condescension and contempt that the Beatles evoked in the mainstream media. "Perplexed and horrified adults . . . knew on some level what they were witnessing: a very public unleashing of sublimated female sexual energy. But they were also seeing something more: . . . the first mass outburst of the Sixties to feature women—in this case, girls. This was terrifying—and it was a premonition."

Beginning with the next day's newspapers, those "perplexed and horrified adults" rendered their opinions. John Horn, in the *New York Herald Tribune,* wrote of the Beatles as they "crawled over the home screen on CBS-TV's *Ed Sullivan Show* last night. Without their shaggy-dog moptops and their sensational buildup," he declared, "they would be four nice boys with a total of one weak voice and one weak beat that rolls more than it rocks. . . . Talentwise, as they say on Madison Ave., the Beatles seem to be 75 per cent publicity, 20 per cent haircut, and 5 per cent lilting lament. They're really a magic act that owes less to Britain than to Barnum."

In the *New York Times,* Jack Gould, in his obligatory reference to the Beatles' hair, said that they "borrow[ed] the square hairdo used every morning on television by Captain Kangaroo." Professing boredom with the whole affair, Gould declared wearily, "Televised Beatlemania appeared to be a fine mass placebo, and thanks are undoubtedly due Britain for a recess in winter's routine. Last night's sedate anticlimax speaks well for continuing British-American understanding. The British always were much more strict with children."

Meanwhile, in Washington, where the Beatles were headed next, Bernie Harrison reported in the *Star* that on their Sullivan appearance, the Beatles "offered about six of their hit numbers, all of which sounded the same. If it weren't for the screams from the audience, they would have put me to sleep. They illustrate the rule which reads that talent is not only unimportant but undesirable in any act aimed like an arrow for the pocketbooks of Young America." The *Washington Post*'s Lawrence Laurent lamented that "our adolescents don't know the difference between parody and the real thing." The Beatles, he wrote, were "imported hillbillies who look like sheep dogs and sound like alley cats in agony."

But along with the critical slams, the Monday-morning media also reported the stunning news that, according to the national Nielsen ratings, *The Ed Sullivan Show* had achieved a score of 44.6. That meant that 73,900,000 Americans had tuned in to watch the Beatles—a figure that represented the largest audience in television history up to that time. In New York City, the Nielsen number was 58.8, indicating that 75 percent of the television sets in use at eight o'clock Sunday night were tuned to Ed Sullivan. By comparison, the latest Nielsen rating in New York for the country's top-rated TV program, *The Beverly Hillbillies,* was 42.9.

Such was the nationwide fascination with the Beatles that, so the story goes, crime decreased almost to nothing while the music played. "When the Beatles were on Ed Sullivan," said George Harrison, "even the criminals had a rest for ten minutes." And evangelist Billy Graham broke his own rule of not watching television on the Sabbath, tuning in the Beatles to try to understand his three teenage daughters. After turning off the set, he proclaimed the Beatles symptomatic "of the uncertainty of the times and the confusion about us. They are part of the trend toward escapism. I hope when they get older they will get a haircut."

Meanwhile, the Beatles did their best to enjoy New York, despite being virtual prisoners at the Plaza. After the Sullivan show on Sunday night, they disdained their limos to walk from 53rd Street up to 59th to the Playboy Club (Paul: "The bunnies are even cuter than we are!"), and then headed over to the Peppermint Lounge, the home of the twist, where Ringo danced and the others partied until four o'clock in the morning. On Monday they held another press conference and received a gold record from Capitol president Alan Livingstone to commemorate the sale of a million copies of "I Want to Hold Your Hand." Not surprisingly, Capitol's Dave Dexter was not invited to the ceremony.

The lead story in Tuesday morning's edition of the *Washington Post* began, "The House of Representatives passed the most comprehensive civil rights bill in history last night by a vote of 290 to 130." Also that morning, the *Post*'s Herblock political cartoon depicted a disgruntled Senator Barry Goldwater (who would go on to win the Republican nomination for president later that year but was then struggling for recognition) surrounded by worried advisers. They have placed a Beatles wig on his head and a guitar in his hands and are telling him, "Just an experiment, Senator—at this point, anything's worth a try." A far briefer story, appearing in the entertainment section under the headline "Mercy, Mersey," stated that the Beatles were scheduled to arrive at National Airport that afternoon at 1:53 via American Airlines flight 241 for their first-ever American concert, an event, said the *Post*, that was "totally, completely, utterly sold out."

But more than eight inches of snow had blanketed the Atlantic Coast region, and all flights into and out of Washington were canceled. Brian Epstein had to scramble to find alternate transportation, and shortly before noon the Beatles left New York's Pennsylvania Station aboard an express train called the Congressman, to which had been added an old Richmond, Fredericksburg, and Potomac Railroad sleeping car called the King George. The journey down to D.C. was far more relaxed and enjoyable for the Beatles than the flight to New York had been. They strolled through the cars signing autographs for passengers and railroad personnel alike. In the King George they clowned for the ever-present cameramen and endured the adoring presence of DJ Murray the K, who had tagged along from New York and would manage to dog them throughout their stay in America. For the benefit, and at the expense, of the reporters, Ringo strung about a dozen cameras around his neck and pushed his way importantly through the car, calling out, "Press! Exclusive!" George donned a porter's hat and coat and walked up and down with cans of Coke and 7-Up on a tray. Paul and John sat contentedly, smoking and gazing out the windows at the wintry scene that unfolded as they rumbled south. Cynthia Lennon made the trip in virtual silence, wearing a black wig in an attempt at anonymity.

It was still snowing when the train arrived at Washington's Union Station at 3:09 P.M. The Beatles made their way down the platform amid a swirl of snowflakes and bursts of flashbulbs. Three thousand young people, some of them gathered beneath a banner proclaiming "WWDC Welcomes the Beatles!" and some of them attempting to scale barred security gates, roared out a welcome.

WWDC's Carroll James, who had been the first to broadcast "I Want to Hold Your Hand," received his reward when the Beatles agreed to an interview at the station. James spent his time with them asking such penetrating questions as, "Do you like cricket?" "Do you like drinking tea?" "Do you like fish and chips?"—evidently doing his best to establish the fact that the Beatles were indeed English. But he also ushered a thrilled Marsha Albert into the studio to meet the band she had helped introduce to America.

That night at eight-thirty, the Beatles gave their first concert on American soil at a building just a few blocks north of Union Station known at the time as the Washington Coliseum. Built in 1941 by Miguel Uline for the Washington Lions of the Eastern Hockey League, and operated for years as the Uline Arena, the Coliseum had seen hockey games, figure skating, boxing and wrestling matches, and midget auto racing. It was also the site of political gatherings such as a "Fight for Freedom" rally a month before the Japanese attack on Pearl Harbor and a speech by the Nation of Islam founder Elijah Muhammad in 1959. In recent years the old arena, surrounded by rusting barbed wire, has served as a trash transfer station, and as the wrecking balls were being readied to pummel it to powder in the autumn of 2003, nearly everyone in

Washington agreed that the most celebrated date in the building's history was February 11, 1964.

Also on the bill with the Beatles that night were some pretty high-profile musicians: Tommy Roe, the Chiffons, Little Anthony and the Imperials, and Jay and the Americans, as well as a young woman named Donna Lynne, who sang her current hit, "My Boyfriend Has a Beatle Haircut." Eight thousand ninety-two fans turned out, paying for tickets that were priced at $2, $3, and $4. They made an immense racket, causing one of the 362 police officers on duty to stick .38 caliber bullets in his ears to try to ward off the sound of screaming. The Beatles played in the center of the Coliseum, surrounded by their fans, and during their forty-minute, twelve-song set they had to keep rotating their microphones, amplifiers, and Ringo's drums around the small stage to try to please everyone. They sang all their hits and also revived some great moments from their Hamburg days, including "Roll Over Beethoven" and "Long Tall Sally." The band had to endure a nearly constant barrage of jelly beans, flashbulbs, and hair rollers hurled at them from all four sides. "M'God!" said Ringo. "They hurt! They felt just like hail-stones." It was hot, the mikes and amps didn't work so well, and it was hard to hear above the constant din, but afterward Paul declared the show among their most excit-ing ever.

At twelve forty-five in the morning the Beatles arrived at the British Embassy on Washington's Massachusetts Avenue for what would turn out to be their last diplomatic event. They were wary of such gatherings from the start and decided to have some fun with the British ambassador to America, David Ormsby-Gore. When they arrived in the embassy's grand foyer, Ormsby-Gore extended his hand and said cordially, "Welcome, John."

"I'm not John," said John. "I'm Charlie. That's John."

"Welcome, John," repeated the ambassador, extending his hand to George.

"I'm not John," said George. "I'm Frank. That's John," pointing to Ringo. The evening at the embassy was off and running.

The Beatles had arrived at the end of a fashionable benefit dance in honor of something called Junior Village and the National Society for the Prevention of Cruelty to Children, one of Lady Ormsby-Gore's pet charities. As reported by the *Washington Post*'s Judith Martin (years before she became known as Miss Manners), the embassy was surrounded by police to keep at bay yet another horde of teenagers. When the crowd inside the embassy surged forward to meet the Beatles, whom one stately dowager called "those darling little baby boys," Martin asked Ringo if he had felt at all threatened by the fans at the Coliseum. "Much more likely to get trampled here," he replied.

And indeed the scene soon turned ugly. A snooty embassy official began thrusting pieces of paper at the Beatles for them to autograph. When John protested, he was told icily, "You'll sign this and like it." John was all for leaving that moment, but Ringo calmed him down and began signing autographs himself. Just then a woman pulled a pair of cuticle scissors from her handbag and snipped off a lock of Ringo's hair. That really set John off.

"We were supposed to put up with all sorts of shit from Lord Mayors and their wives," he raged, "and be touched and pawed like in *A Hard Day's Night,* only a million times more. At the British Embassy in Washington, some bloody animal cut Ringo's hair. I walked out, swearing at all of them. I just left in the middle of it."

The others remained long enough to hand out raffle prizes for the charity and then left for a short night at the Shoreham Hotel. Brian Epstein was livid at the treatment they had received and resolved that from then on the Beatles would attend no more official government functions. The reaction in England was also one of outrage, with a member of Parliament demanding a full report from Foreign Secretary R. A. Butler. The following Sunday's *London Express* contained an editorial declaring that the current crop of British diplomats had a lot to learn. "If that's the type we are sending to Washington, it doesn't seem a very good advertisement for Britain. Indeed, if we brought them home and left the Beatles in their place, our diplomacy with America might be improved." That brought an immediate response from the *New York Herald Tribune:* "Oh, No You Don't," ran the headline.

Indeed, the media reaction to the Beatles' visit to Washington was one of derision. The *Post's* review of their concert on Tuesday night made the undeniable point that the band's music was hard to hear above the roar of the crowd but went on to declare that while the Beatles' "voices are a bit thin, they possess the quality of semi-hysteria so necessary for this kind of performance. Also, they sweat and smile a lot."

An op-ed piece in the *Post* headlined "The Beatles Blues" opined, "Just thinking about the Beatles seems to induce mental disturbance. They have a commonplace, rather dull act, about as exciting as Fink's Mules." The *Washington Star,* in an editorial titled "They Bug Us," declared, "Their musical talent is minimal. Their weird hair style is merely a combination of the beehive and the Hamlet, or 'little moron,' hairdo. Months ago, the Star editorially expressed thanks that we had nothing like the Beatles in this country. We're still thankful for that. We may never have produced a Shakespeare. But we never produced a Beatle, either."

On Wednesday morning, February 12, the Beatles left the Shoreham in a group of three limousines and a single police car, hurtled up Capitol Hill for a brief photo session, and then raced down the hill to Union Station, where they boarded a train for New York five minutes before it was due to depart. Paul stood in the caboose waving a red brakeman's flag as the train pulled out at 11:46 A.M., leaving behind another torrent of young fans.

Thousands more fans awaited their arrival at Pennsylvania Station in New York. "I've never seen anything like it, and I was here when Castro arrived, when Khrushchev came in, but this topped them all," a veteran Penn employee told the *Herald Tribune.* To avoid the crush, police escorted the Beatles off the train shortly before it reached the station and spirited them up a freight elevator. They then took another set of limos back to the Plaza Hotel. At least a dozen teenage girls were hurt in the subsequent melee set off when the Beatles' train pulled in at three-thirty, and the fans found it empty of their heroes.

Yet another immense crowd of young people awaited the arrival of the Beatles at the Plaza. As their limos pulled up to the hotel from the south, a second motorcade attempted to negotiate its way through the throng but was forced to come to a halt a hundred yards from the Plaza's entrance. Its main occupant had to push his way, salmonlike, up the river of humanity to register at the front desk. Such was the excitement over the imminent arrival of the Beatles that no one seemed to notice the presence of Attorney General Robert F. Kennedy.

At about the same time, a concert of American classical music, sponsored by radio station WNYC, was being presented at Carnegie Hall, in part to mark the Lincoln's Birthday holiday. To the surprise of even the most hopeful organizers of the concert, the venerable hall at 57th Street and Seventh Avenue was packed, giving rise to a brief sense of optimism that this music, some of it quite new and challenging, had found an enthusiastic audience. But an explanation for the healthy turnout came shortly after the concert ended, when thirty special policemen hired by Sid Bernstein swept through the hall and found, hiding under seats, dozens of resourceful Beatle fans who had bought tickets for the WNYC show hoping to sneak into that evening's concerts. They were politely but firmly shown the door.

By six o'clock that evening police estimated that there were about five thousand people in the streets outside Carnegie, only some with precious tickets—priced from $3.00 to $5.50—to the two concerts that Bernstein had booked months before. A small contigent of about fifteen young men stood near the 57th Street entrance holding hostile signs bearing messages such as "Exterminate the Beatles!" Shortly after the first concert started, they were rushed by a group of teenage girls, who managed to destroy a few of the signs before being hauled away by the authorities.

Inside the hall, more than twenty-nine hundred fans were in attendance, about one hundred fifty of whom were seated on stage. Backstage, the Beatles were visited by Shirley Bassey, who later that year would have a number-one hit of her own with the title song to the hit James Bond movie *Goldfinger.* An American folk group called the Briarwoods performed the unenviable task of opening the show, but at seven-forty-five the Beatles ran onto the stage to a roar of delight. They played a dozen songs in thirty-four minutes and then sprinted back to the safety of the dressing rooms. The hall was swept for stragglers, and the second concert began at a little after nine-thirty. The Beatles played their same thirty-four-minute set, the screams were just as loud (John once tried to calm every-one down by hollering "Shut up!"), and the night was over. Filing out into the clogged and happy streets, Mrs. Nelson Rockefeller, the wife of New York's governor, who attended the concert with two of her children, told a reporter, "I loved it. They were marvelous, they have a lot of talent. It was one of the most extraordinary things I've ever seen."

In expressing such a positive reaction, Mrs. Rockefeller was sailing against the current of opinion that carried along most adult observers of the Beatles. But less than forty-eight hours later, on the same Carnegie Hall stage, the great conductor Leopold Stokowski expressed his admiration for the Beatles, both as musicians and as messengers of joy. He had conducted the American Symphony Orchestra in music by Beethoven and Stravinsky for an audience of junior high school students from all five of New York City's boroughs. After the concert he spoke with the kids about the power of music and with their teachers about his respect for the Beatles. "They give the teen-agers something that thrills them, a vision," said Stokowski. "The boys and girls of this age are young men and women looking for something in life that can't always be found, a *joie de vivre*. Life is changing all the time. We are all looking for a vision of the ecstasy of life. I am, too." When he uttered those words, Leopold Stokowski was eighty-one years old.

But the mainstream criticism was in full force when the Beatles flew to Miami on Thursday afternoon. The *Miami Herald* set the tone by writing, "For the information of the young and deranged, these wailing weirdies will disembark from National Airlines Flight 11 at 3:55 P.M." During the flight from New York, the "weirdies" cheerfully signed more than two hundred autographs for the eighty passengers on board the airplane. When the National DC-8 pulled up to Gate 27 of Miami International Airport, a crowd of about seven thousand teenagers, mostly girls, did their best to welcome the Beatles to Florida. There were the usual shrieks of joy, but this time there was a lot more damage to airport property. In all the excitement, a plate-glass door was shattered, twenty-three windows were broken, a dozen fiberglass-and-fabric chairs were torn up, five enormous tub-sized sand-filled ashtrays were overturned, and seven young people were treated for cuts and bruises.

The kids had been told the arrival time of the Beatles' flight, not only by the snide reporter of the *Herald,* but repeatedly by the dueling Miami radio stations WFUN and WQAM. They swarmed the arrival gate and stood gleefully on airline countertops in an effort to catch a glimpse of the band. One young man risked more serious injury when he leaped from an airport observation deck down to the tarmac, where, temporarily stunned by the impact, he was promptly taken into custody. Damage to the airport was estimated at two thousand dollars.

The authorities were not amused. "If I ever caught my kid out here," a sweating cop swore, "I'd beat the hell out of her. This is disgusting!" And Clifford E. Mitchell, the administrative assistant to the Dade County superintendent of schools, insisted publicly that all kids who played hooky on Thursday afternoon would be required to make up the time lost in after-school sessions the following week.

The Beatles were hustled through the mob to the usual waiting limos that maneuvered through a four-mile-long traffic jam caused by all the commotion at the airport and then drove them to the Deauville Hotel in Miami Beach, site of the second Ed Sullivan broadcast on Sunday the sixteenth. At the hotel, they met the press once again. A woman reporter asked, "What are you doing tonight?" George responded, "I don't know. What are you doing?"

Reporter: "What will you do about the mobs when you go in the water?"
Ringo: "Use swimming policemen."
Reporter: "Will your wife hold a press conference?
John: "No, but you can come to tea."
Reporter: "Who writes the music?"
John: "What music?"
Reporter: "Do you regret your loss of freedom?"
Paul: "Not really. We never went out that much before anyway. We're not great outdoor types."

After the press conference broke up, the Beatles and dozens of others hurried off to the hotel elevators. Ringo recognized a young woman singer and invited her into the elevator with him. Later a reporter asked him who she was. "Just a girl I know," he replied. "What's her last name?" the reporter persisted. Said Ringo, "I don't know her *that* well."

The next two days were a warm and welcome respite from the nonstop activity of the previous week. There were brief rehearsals for Sunday's Sullivan show on Friday and Saturday and a photo shoot with a photographer from *Life* magazine in the swimming pool at the home of a Capitol Records executive, but most of the time the Beatles just enjoyed the sun and fun of Miami Beach. Late on Thursday night, they stopped in at the Peppermint Lounge, caught the Coasters in concert at the Mau Mau

Lounge, and then headed up the strip to the Wreck Bar of the Castaways Motel, returning to their rooms at the Deauville at two-thirty in the morning. On Friday afternoon they boarded a ninety-five-foot yacht called the *Southern Trail,* generously put at their disposal by the owner of the Castro Convertible Bed Company. The boys water-skied, splashed in the warm waters of the Atlantic, and dozed in the sun. They relaxed and enjoyed themselves enormously.

"Miami was like paradise," recalled Paul. "We had never been anywhere where there were palm trees. We were real tourists, we had our Pentax cameras and took a lot of pictures. We'd never seen a policeman with a gun, either, and those Miami cops did look pretty groovy. I think, though, that we were hanging out with Mafiosi. There was a critic giving us a hard time in the press. George Martin and Brian Epstein were discussing it when a big heavy guy came up and said, 'Mr. Epstein, you want we should fix this guy?' That was the kind of crowd we were in. But we didn't know that—we just saw a nice man with a pool and a yacht."

The staff of *The Ed Sullivan Show* set up for Sunday night's program in the Deauville Hotel's Napoleon Room, the largest of the hotel's three ballrooms. On Sunday afternoon, the Beatles gave a dress rehearsal performance for about twenty-five hundred mostly young fans, and all went well. But then came the live broadcast that evening, and pandemonium. CBS had printed and distributed thirty-five hundred tickets to the show, but the capacity of the Napoleon Room was slightly under twenty-six hundred.

When the Napoleon doors swung open at seven o'clock that evening, a line of ticket holders snaked five abreast for more than two hundred yards through the hotel lobby and for an extra two blocks outside the hotel. The doors closed at seven-fifty to allow Ed Sullivan to warm up the crowd, and nearly a thousand people holding apparently valid tickets were left outside in the lobby, fuming. These were not happy teenagers, but frustrated adults. The *Miami Herald* reported the next day that "the oldsters outdid the kids in mobbing *The Ed Sullivan Show*. A man in a white dinner jacket threw a wicked right at a young usher. A grandmother hammered a head with her high heels in her hand." A woman who managed to get inside the Napoleon Room just minutes before the doors closed told a reporter, "You don't know what's going on out there. You'd think it was life or death."

But it wasn't just spectators who had a hard time getting in. Five minutes before airtime, the Beatles came down from their rooms on the twelfth floor, stepped gingerly out of the elevator, and found an angry herd of humanity milling about between them and the Napoleon Room. They were scheduled to open the show, but there was no way to get to the set except through the crowd. After attempting to edge their way forward politely and getting nowhere, the Beatles accepted the assistance of a flying wedge of those groovy gun-toting Miami cops, who burst through the throng, scattering bodies left and right. With seconds to spare before their cue, the Beatles took their places behind a curtain on the Napoleon Room's makeshift stage.

Unbeknownst to either them or Ed Sullivan, yet another difficulty had arisen. A crowd of kids, at least as large as the crowd of their elders in the lobby, had gathered in the hotel parking lot and noticed the CBS control truck. Realizing that there was no way they could get in to see the show live, they apparently decided to watch the broadcast on the truck's monitors. Bill Bohnert remembers glancing out the windows just in time to see the leading wave of the crowd crashing forward, ready to engulf the truck. Reacting quickly, Bohnert dived across the console and managed to bolt the doors just in time. Throughout the broadcast, the kids climbed all over the truck, shaking it from side to side, and Bohnert feared that a cable or two might be unplugged, interrupting the feed back to New York. But luckily everything remained intact and the show went on.

It opened with a prerecorded shot of horses galloping down the stretch run of Miami's Hialeah Race Track. George Fenniman, for many years Groucho Marx's sidekick on the TV show *You Bet Your Life,* stood in the track's infield to announce that the program was sponsored by Lipton Tea. Then, back at the Deauville, Ed Sullivan strolled out to announce, "Last Sunday on our show in New York the Beatles played to the greatest television audience that's ever been assembled in the history of American TV. Now tonight, here in Miamuh Beach, again the Beatles face a record-busting audience. Ladies and gentlemen, here are four of the nicest youngsters we've ever had on our stage. . . . The Beatles, bring 'em on out . . ."

The curtains parted and out stepped John, Paul, and

George, with Ringo perched on his drum platform, the television audience unaware of how recently they had arrived there. In their first set, the Beatles performed "She Loves You," "This Boy," and "All My Loving." All the mikes worked, and the band sounded relaxed and tight. During "This Boy," John threw in a few extra falsetto notes and nearly cracked himself up. During Paul's intro to "All My Loving," he mentioned their new album on Capitol Records and John asked loudly, in mock horror, "Can you say that?" The days of rest had certainly mellowed them.

The audience seemed mellow as well, or maybe it was just that many more older folks were gathered in the Napoleon Room that night. There were screams, of course, but the sense of barely controlled exuberance, such a vital part of the previous week's show, was absent.

After the Beatles had ducked back behind the curtain, Ed Sullivan recognized Sonny Liston, the heavyweight boxer who was due to fight the young challenger Cassius Clay in Miami on February 25, and asked him to stand and take a bow. The comedy team of Marty ("Hello dere") Allen and Steve Rossi, the singer Mitzi Gaynor, the comedian Myron Cohen, and four Swiss acrobats known as the Nerveless Knocks performed, and then the Beatles came out once more.

They played "I Saw Her Standing There," "From Me to You," and, with Paul reviving his lame joke from the Royal Command Performance—"This next song was recorded by our favorite American group, Sophie Tucker"—"I Want to Hold Your Hand." Again they sounded utterly relaxed and confident. When they'd finished, Ed Sullivan invited them to stage right and told them, "Richard Rodgers, one of America's greatest composers, wanted me to tell you that he's one of your most rabid fans . . . and that goes for me, too!"

There was more good ratings news for Sullivan the next morning. Though the numbers were not quite as huge as for the previous week's show, the broadcast from Miami managed a 44.2 Nielsen rating, or an audience of seventy million viewers.

The Beatles had originally planned to fly home to London on Monday the seventeenth, but the sun proved so alluring that they put off their return until the end of the week. They spent much of their time fishing, waterskiing, and boating. Ringo borrowed a speedboat and managed to damage the owner's slip when he brought the craft back in too quickly. On Tuesday, one set of icons from the 1960s met another when the Beatles visited the gym where Cassius Clay (not yet Muhammad Ali) was training for his fight with Sonny Liston. They climbed into the ring with Clay, and photographer Harry Benson snapped a memorable image of the fighter apparently knocking out all four of them with a single punch. Clay composed one of his famous bits of doggerel for the occasion, proclaiming, "When Sonny Liston picks up the papers and sees that the Beatles came to see me/He will become so angry that I will knock him out in three." As the Beatles left the gym, a reporter asked John who he liked in the upcoming fight. "Louis Armstrong," he replied.

On Friday the twenty-first, they returned home. Maintaining a consistent tone until the end, the *Miami Herald* reported, "The plague of the Beatles has lifted. After an eight-day local infestation, the Liverpudlian dandies caught a jet from Miami for New York and London, as five-hundred-odd adolescent females here bid them a blubbering bye-bye." In New York, the *Herald Tribune* declared that their departure from Kennedy Airport "was even more triumphant and hysterical than their arrival. Police lines were stormed. Patrolmen were injured. Girls fainted." Estimates of the crowd again approached ten thousand people. As the Beatles left their Eastern Air Lines jet from Miami to transfer to the Pan Am plane that would wing them home to England, they were briefly visible to the fans. The young people surged forward along the observation deck, and several Port Authority patrolmen suffered injuries to their legs and chests while trying to hold them back. With a final flurry of waves and smiles, the Beatles disappeared.

Looking back on those tumultuous two weeks many years later, George Harrison said, "I didn't think beyond the moment during that U.S. trip. I wasn't really aware of any change-over in our fame. I don't think I looked to the future much. We just enjoyed the novelty of 'conquering' America." But one of his mates did look ahead and didn't like what he saw. After the second *Ed Sullivan Show*, there was a sit-down dinner party for the cast and crew, held in the Deauville Hotel's main dining room. Associate director John Moffitt found himself at a table with Ringo, who looked very downhearted even as he consumed great quantities of lobster and beef. When Moffitt asked him what was wrong, Ringo paused, and then with a faraway look in his eyes said, "This has just been the most brilliant week. How in the world are we ever going to top this? I'm sure it's all going to be downhill from here."

10

The Children of
Bishop Martin

He needn't have worried, of course.

By the end of 1964, the Beatles had released two more albums (*A Hard Day's Night* and *Beatles for Sale*) and their first film (*A Hard Day's Night*, directed by Richard Lester). They had performed in Europe, in Hong Kong, in Australia and New Zealand, and once more in North America, giving thirty-one performances in twenty-four cities in the United States and Canada over a period of thirty-two days. And their popularity just kept growing. On April 4, the Beatles held down the first five places on the Billboard "Hot 100" chart: number one was their newest single, "Can't Buy Me Love," followed by "Twist and Shout," "She Loves You," "I Want to Hold Your Hand," and "Please Please Me." No band or individual had ever done anything like that before, and no one has done it since.

By the end of the decade, the Beatles would issue a total

of twelve original albums, including the double "White Album," and more than two dozen singles. At the heart of their output was a magnificent collection of 184 original songs, the vast majority by Lennon and McCartney but including some wonderful contributions from George and even a couple by Ringo. But the band had become a product of the recording studio, not the live concert stage. After a concert in San Francisco's Candlestick Park on August 29, 1966, the Beatles never again performed for a paying audience. The demands of their worldwide schedule had become exhausting, musically counterproductive, and, thanks to an encounter with President Marcos's security goons in the Philippines, dangerous. The Beatles were now prisoners of their own success and wanted no more of it. George lamented, "Foxes have holes and birds have nests, but Beatles have nowhere to lay their heads." John was more succinct: "We're going to remain normal if it kills us."

But the Beatles were anything but normal; they were the greatest band and the most influential cultural force of the decade that became synonymous with their name. Their arrival in America in 1964 was an earthquake, and we continue to feel its aftershocks forty years later.

The Beatles were great artists, and their most important influence was musical. To begin with, their sound and style represented a unique synthesis of many genres—from early rock 'n' roll, blues, and country music to traditional English music hall—with their own interests and passions. Roger McGuinn of the Byrds, a great American band that was hugely inspired by the Beatles, says that the English band "connected the dots between folk music and rock music" in a manner that had never before been attempted. Their harmonies, both instrumental and vocal; the ringing sounds of their guitars; their constant devotion to experimentation with new chords and rhythms and unusual sonic sources from electronic feedback to backward tapes; and, especially in their later songs, the powerful imagery of their words set a standard of musicality that delighted and challenged their fans and raised the bar for their competitors.

The Beatles, along with Bob Dylan—born in 1941, a year after John Lennon and a year before Paul McCartney—helped usher in the great age of the singer-songwriter. Before the Beatles came along, pop musicians rarely sang their own songs; neither Frank Sinatra nor Elvis Presley was a composer. After the Beatles, groups were expected to perform their own material; relying exclusively on cover songs was a sure sign of a second-rate band.

The Beatles set such a high standard that many musicians found it impossible to compete and quietly retired to some other line of work. Pop stars who enjoyed great success in 1962 and 1963—Neil Sedaka, Del Shannon, Bobby Vinton, Bobby Vee, Dick and Dee-Dee, and the Dixie Cups—were has-beens by the end of 1964, prematurely bound for the oldies section in record shops across the country. As wildman rocker Jerry Lee Lewis observed, "The Beatles cut 'em all down like wheat before the sickle."

The Beatles also inspired and brought to life a lot of music. Within two years such American bands as the Byrds and the Monkees, who owed their sound and their look to the Beatles, were climbing the charts. And of course the Beatles were the opening salvo in the celebrated British Invasion; thanks to them the Rolling Stones, the Who, the Animals, the Zombies, the Kinks, the Dave Clark Five, Herman's Hermits, Manfred Mann, Peter and Gordon, Chad and Jeremy, the Hollies, Freddie and the Dreamers, and Liverpool's own Gerry and the Pacemakers found a welcome home in America.

Also thanks to the Beatles, rock 'n' roll was soon no longer the province of production houses and label managers. The Beatles, assisted by George Martin, insisted on complete control over their songs and albums; not mere "talent" anymore, the musician as artist became a firmly established and widely accepted concept. Within a few years, such figures as Jimi Hendrix, Janis Joplin, Stephen Stills, Eric Clapton, and Carlos Santana were recognized as important contributors to a vibrant and exciting musical culture. Rock 'n' roll truly was here to stay.

Ironically, because the Beatles eventually retreated to the studio to make their magic, they also forever altered the size and scope of touring. Nobody thought of booking a ballpark for a band in 1963, but once the Beatles attracted fifty-five thousand people to Shea Stadium, the age of the stadium rock concert had begun.

The Beatles also profoundly affected the business of transmitting music, both via radio and recordings. Top-40 radio was a tired medium at the end of 1963, having experienced nothing new since the arrival of Elvis Presley and the dawning of rock 'n' roll itself eight years earlier. But from the moment the Beatles' Pan Am jet touched down at Kennedy Airport, American radio was transformed. Stations from coast to coast realized that they now had to sound as hip and fresh as the new music they were broadcasting and moved quickly to reinvent their image, adding jingles, improved production values, and English slang to their daily patter. Album sales boomed. Before the advent of the Beatles, only Lawrence Welk or Frank Sinatra or the occasional Broadway show sold record albums in great numbers; rock 'n' roll was enjoyed at forty-five revolutions per minute. But the Beatles' legions of fans had to have every song the boys recorded, and the way to do that was to buy their albums. As a result, electronics sales went up as well, as people needed newer and better equipment to fully experience the Beatles' increasingly complex studio work.

The arrival of the Beatles in 1964 also signaled the start of serious rock journalism in America. Such phenomena as the enormous crowds who greeted the band at the airports in New York and Miami, the crush of the boys' first press conferences, and the unheard-of ratings recorded by *The Ed Sullivan Show* had to be taken seriously, and rock 'n' roll, largely ignored by the mainstream press in 1963, suddenly became newsworthy. As its coverage increased, some people began to perceive that rock was dangerous and posed a cultural threat.

At first it was all in fun, as Ace Hardware offered special cans of the insect repellent Raid to "help stamp out the Beatles." But in March 1966, John Lennon gave an interview to his friend Maureen Cleave of the *London Evening Standard*. One of the topics covered was the state of contemporary religion, and John declared that Christianity had lost so many followers recently that the Beatles "are more popular than Jesus now. I don't know which will go first—rock 'n' roll or Christianity."

There was virtually no reaction to John's comments in England, but in late July, just before the Beatles came to America for what would be their last concert tour, an American magazine republished the interview. Christian fundamentalist groups reacted with outrage. A disc jockey in Birmingham, Alabama, organized an immediate boycott of the Beatles' songs and used the airwaves to broadcast plans for what became the first of several ritualistic burnings of their albums. Beatles records were banned from the airways of the South African Broadcasting Corporation, a ban that lasted until after the band's breakup. A gap had opened up between those who adored the Beatles and those who feared them.

There have been conflicts between the generations since the days of Adam and Cain, and in many ways the musical generation gap of the 1960s was no different from the Sinatra-inspired gap of the bobby-soxed 1940s or the Elvis gap of the 1950s. But other forces were at work when the Beatles sang their songs of love, and a different sort of gap opened, narrow at first, but widening into an almost unbridgeable chasm by the end of the decade.

In the same week of February 1964 that the *Washington Post* wrote condescendingly of the Beatles' first American concert at the Washington Coliseum, the *New York Times* ran a story that quoted one of President Johnson's most influential cabinet members: "Secretary of State Dean Rusk said today that he had 'no doubt' about the long-range success of efforts to help South Vietnam survive Communist guerrilla attacks and subversion. Mr. Rusk said South Vietnam had the resources and the will 'to get this job done.' He implied that there was no need for a greater involvement by the United States."

More stories about Vietnam appeared in the pages of America's newspapers that month: guerrillas bombed a ballpark in Saigon, killing two American GIs; the government of South Vietnam was reorganized following two coups d'état; and Senator Goldwater opined that greater American resources should be spent to meet the Communist menace.

In November 1964, President Johnson won a landslide election victory built in part on his pledge of "restraint" where Vietnam was concerned. Four years later, that "restraint" had led to more than half a million American soldiers in Vietnam.

So as our generation came to consciousness, we came to realize that much of the older generation had gotten the two most important calls of the Sixties wrong: the Beatles and Vietnam. One was a decidedly deadlier mistake, of course, but we also took cultural matters seriously. The same adult authority figures who told us kids that the Beatles were "shaggy shriekers" and "wailing weirdies" whose music was either boring or incomprehensible would soon encourage us to risk our lives and limbs in Vietnam. If they're so wrong about the Beatles, we asked ourselves, how can we trust them to make the right decisions regarding Vietnam? As it turned out, of course, we couldn't. After a while it became an article of faith not to "trust anyone over thirty."

Of course, that gap, widely believed to be generational,

was always more about the distance that separated two very different ways of looking at the world. One way preferred the maintenance of order and the established hierarchies of race, sex, class, and international spheres of influence. The other questioned all the assumptions of the first way.

From Holden Caulfield fearing that phonies were coming in the window to Sal Paradise searching for kicks and truth on the road, young people adopted heroes who struggled to achieve a vision of the world that emphasized more than the American dream of suck-cess, as Bob Dylan sang. We learned early on that we could trust the Beatles, because they rewarded our trust with great music and with honesty and integrity. On their second visit to America, in September of 1964, they announced that they would not perform at the Gator Bowl in Jacksonville, Florida, if, as they'd heard, the audience would be segregated. A few years later, they proclaimed their opposition to the war in Vietnam.

But, as always, it was primarily the integrity of their music that dazzled us. Looking back on his earliest collaborations with John Lennon, Paul McCartney said, "It was great because instead of looking into my own mind for a song I could see John playing—as if he were holding a mirror to what I was doing." A mirror is a marvelous image, and one that helps explain the complicated yet essential relationship between the Beatles and their fans during the turbulent, heady days of the Sixties.

On the one hand, a mirror reflects, and by looking at the Beatles we could see the outward manifestations of the times, the changes in hair and clothes and attitudes that were both superficial and profound, in the manner of that complicated decade. The arrival of the Beatles in 1964 signaled the onset of long hair for men; when they grew beards and mustaches in 1966, so did young men around the world; when they appeared on the cover of their epochal album *Sgt. Pepper's Lonely Hearts Club Band* wearing colorful psychedelic uniforms just as the Summer of Love of 1967 was starting, it marked the moment when hippie fashions and mores moved from the outer fringes of society to mainstream suburbia. The Beatles made no secret of their use of marijuana and LSD, both for recreation and for inspiration, and fans eagerly accepted the invitation at the end of "A Day in the Life": "I'd love to turn you on." The Beatles themselves challenged the notion that they led the way in changing the world's attitudes toward hair and clothes and drugs, saying that they were merely moving with the times. That they reflected the times clearly, however, there can be no doubt.

But mirrors are also an entryway into new lands both rich and strange, from John's beloved Alice passing through the looking glass to Jean Cocteau's use of mirrors as mesmerizing symbols of the doors of perception. The Beatles invited us to join them on a magical journey of music, of ideas, and of the deepest emotions. They were musical explorers who led their followers to new artistic and spiritual places. And as they broadened the boundaries of our musical experiences, they encouraged us to expand other horizons in our lives. They brought us unbridled joy and excitement in their early songs. Then they extended and deepened our understanding of popular music, adding instruments, shadings, meanings, length and breadth and depth, borrowing from influences as diverse as Indian ragas, the *Tibetan Book of the Dead,* and the English music hall. If they wouldn't restrict themselves to the accepted limits of a three-minute pop ballad, why should we lower our sights or rein in our ambitions and dreams? The Beatles started out great and only got better; what a magnificent example to emulate!

That's an aspect of their appeal that sometimes gets ignored. By February 1964 the Beatles had played hard for four years and countless hours under circumstances that ranged from merely challenging to physically taxing and occasionally dangerous. Theirs was an act, and an art, that had been honed and polished and burnished and developed as the boys themselves grew and matured. They had worked hard.

We didn't know all that when we first met the Beatles. We just listened and screamed. But part of what we loved, though we weren't aware of it, was the work and the sweat and the sleepless nights and the pills and the booze and the grit and rage of the Reeperbahn. That was one of the sources of their passion, and that, along with the music, was what moved us so.

Part of what was so moving about the music was its constant evolution. Every Beatles album was in some way an advancement over the previous one. That, too, mirrored the ethos of the Sixties. It was an article of faith that life would get better, problems would be solved, injustice would be overcome, humankind would escape the gravitational pull of the earth and land on the distant moon. With the Beatles' ever-expanding music sounding a magnificent accompaniment, it was a time of hope and optimism when all things seemed possible, when we knew for certain that all we really did need was love. Those who couldn't hear the music then and lack the heart to hear it now continue desperately to mock and try to discredit the Sixties, apparently still hurt and angry about how wrong they were then and fearful of the era's lasting power. But we who truly believed then still believe, and yearn anew for inspiration.

The United States remains a young country among the nations of the world, and youthfulness has always been an American ideal. A youth culture had already sprung up in the 1950s, when rock 'n' roll was born; the Pepsi Generation—"for those who think young"—had already been anointed by Madison Avenue in 1964. But the arrival of the Beatles certainly hastened the transformation of American society—or at least its coverage by the mass media—into one that worshipped at the altar of golden youth. With so much money being generated by the Beatles, the race was on to discover the next act or fad or fashion that would appeal to young people. The marketers and product developers may not have understood why young people loved the Beatles, but that didn't matter; youth was going to be served, and tidy profits would follow.

As someone who loves Bach, Beethoven, Brahms, and the Beatles, I look with envy and a touch of sadness at the radio page of the *Washington Post* for Sunday, February 9,

1964—the day of the Beatles' bow on *Ed Sullivan*. No fewer than five local radio stations offered classical music programming that day, including live broadcasts from Boston, New York, and Washington's own National Gallery of Art. It was a matter of certainty that great music from the past—sometimes the distant past—should be an honored part of the present. By acquainting ourselves with ancient ideas of knowledge and beauty, we would constantly renew our lives and our souls. Timeless art *mattered*.

In the intervening forty years, of course, an increasing emphasis on what is new and youthful has relegated such ideas to a degree of quaintness on a level with buggy whips and hand-cranked ice cream. Things that require more time to savor or understand are deemed old-fashioned and not worthy of our limited time and attention. In today's Washington, only two terrestrial radio stations offer any classical music programming. Paul McCartney has written music in the classical tradition in the last decade and surely regrets aspects of what has come to pass, but the coming of the Beatles signaled the end of the old order. In retrospect, then, perhaps it's easier to understand the hostility of the Establishment: on some level, it knew it was doomed.

But as much as youth is served in today's marketplace, youth itself, as Shakespeare sang, "is a stuff will not endure." Today, John Lennon and George Harrison are dead and Paul McCartney and Ringo Starr are over sixty years old, still touring, still making music, yet clearly slowing down as they make their inevitable concessions to the calendar. And we who make up the heart of the Beatles

Generation are all past fifty and beginning to come to terms with our own mortality.

Ah, but while individual Beatles are not what they were ("some are dead and some are living"), the Beatles remain forever young. After they broke apart in 1970, the oldest of them thirty years old, they had the good sense never to regroup, except for their clever use of technology to produce two poignant final songs from John Lennon demos for the 1996 *Anthology* series. As a result, nearly everything we have of the Beatles dates from those magical ten years from Hamburg to the Abbey Road sessions. They bloomed brightly with the sun of their inspiration and their youth, and then, like Mozart and Schubert, they left us before their flower faded. The Beatles of Liverpool, in the words of the poet A. E. Housman, who wrote of life in neighboring Shropshire, are "the lads that will never be old." And we, who loved them first when both they and we were young, hold their music ever more dear as with rue our hearts are laden with our advancing age.

Flying into Liverpool's John Lennon Airport (official slogan: "Above Us Only Sky"), I ponder the concentric circles of ownership that surround the Beatles. Later, I visit the Casbah Coffee Club in East Derby and walk down Liverpool's rebuilt Mathew Street to clump down the stairs into the renovated Cavern Club. It's appropriately hot and loud, and ghosts seem to hover in dark corners, momentarily glimpsed among young bodies who dance and dream. This is the inner circle, where the Beatles' earliest

fans came to sweat and scream and witnessed the remark-
able beginnings of an epic journey. Moving outward,
there are the circles of those who heard them in their many
Merseyside concerts, then in England, then in Europe,
then throughout the world.

But there is another series of circles made up of generations, and all of us who met the Beatles when they came to
America in 1964, who stayed with them eagerly as they
grew and astonished us over and over again, and who
remember the Beatles as a present-day phenomenon, feel a
privileged place in that inner circle. Those of us who were
young when the boys were young hold them especially
close with a tight and tender clasp born of ownership. The
Beatles are *ours*.

My dear wife, born in July 1965, a month before the
Beatles played Shea Stadium for the first time, has had to
endure endlessly repetitive tales of what it was like to hear
a new Beatles song, to rush down to the record store to
buy a new Beatles album, to take it home and listen and
learn in wonder and joy. I have told her often (and she
listens lovingly every time) that my first solo drive in the
family car was through the snowy streets of Cleveland in
December 1968 to join my friends at Billy Ginn's house to
listen collectively to the just-released "White Album."
She has told me that she remembers driving with her parents half a day from their small town in eastern Montana
to the bright city lights of Billings, there to buy a new Billy
Joel album. All the way home in the car she would read
the lyrics of the new songs and anticipate how those words
would sound translated into music. "I guess that's what it

was like with you and the Beatles," she says. And I quietly, and with a great deal of satisfaction, say to myself, "No, it wasn't. . . ." She loves the Beatles, too, of course, but she loves them as she loves Bach and Brahms and Benny Goodman: artists of the past who speak to her today, as all great artists do. But those of us who came to consciousness as the Beatles emerged, and who grew as they grew and as they helped us to grow, feel a deeper love, I think—a love laced with that pride of ownership.

In our lives, we loved them more.

Those are my thoughts as, on an uncommonly warm summer day, my last in Liverpool, I once more climb the hill to St. Peter's Church in Woolton. Here, truly, is where it all began, and I pause for a long moment to gaze at the stone marker on the outer wall of the Church Hall that commemorates the meeting of John and Paul on July 6, 1957. Across Church Street is the graveyard, and beyond that the field where the Quarry Men performed at that fateful fete. There beneath the blue suburban skies I stand in silent awe, until a friendly verger emerges from the church to greet me. On hearing that I have come from America to pay homage, he smiles and takes me on a brief tour of the grounds.

Here is the grave of George Toogood Smith, John's uncle. The verger speculates that John must have walked right past the grave on his way from the field to his meeting with Paul. He then shows me the adjacent graves of families named Rigby and McKenzie. The Rigby plot is a large one, and yes, here is the grave of Eleanor Rigby, "beloved wife of Thomas Woods, died 10th October

1939, aged 44 years." The verger tells me that Paul still insists that those names came to him unconsciously.

We hear laughter and turn to see a line of children coming through the far hedge two by two, holding each other by the hand. They are young students of the Bishop Martin Church of England Primary School. The boys are dressed in uniforms of purple shirts and gray shorts, the girls in dresses of white and purple stripes. They smile shyly at us as they file into St. Peter's. The verger shakes my hand and hurries inside after them.

Left alone in the warmth of a perfect summer's day, I turn and gaze down the hill to the southwest, past the blue river Mersey to where I think I see the distant mountains of northern Wales. A lone gull wheels and shrieks overhead and after a few moments flies away, free as a bird.

And then from within St. Peter's Church comes the sound of sweet childish voices. To my amazement and joy, they sing "Octopus's Garden," and then "When I'm Sixty-Four," and then "Eleanor Rigby." The six- and seven-year-old voices are largely devoid of comprehension, but unimaginably moving. With tears in my eyes and a great goofy smile on my face, I lean back against a headstone and listen as the music pours out of the church to mingle momentarily with the warm air above my head before, in my imagination, it heads off down the hill in the direction of my ecstatic gaze, to join the far-off world.

"We would be so happy you and me, no one there to tell us what to do . . ."

"If I'd been out till quarter to three, would you lock the door . . ."

"All the lonely people, where do they all come from . . ."

The little children of Bishop Martin remind me yet again of the timelessness of this magnificent music and of how it is slipping away from us who think we own it. When these sweet children are indeed sixty-four, we who remember the magic of that distant *Ed Sullivan Show* will all be dust. But the music of the Beatles will still live, will go on spreading its joy and its message of hope and love and limitless possibilities, on past distant seasons and the farthest horizons, on and on across the universe.

Acknowledgments

My sincere thanks to many people who have been of great assistance on the long and winding road of this project.

At XM Satellite Radio, I deeply appreciate the immediate enthusiasm with which Hugh Panero, Steve Gavenas, and Steve Harris greeted the news of this opportunity and the speed with which they granted my leave of absence that enabled me to research and write. Thanks to engineer extraordinaire Jim McBean. And a special word of thanks to Lee Abrams for his knowledge, passion, wit, and encouragement.

Thanks to Kitt Allan at Wiley for her belief and advocacy, and to Hana Lane and Marcia Samuels for their perceptive and helpful editing.

Thanks to the following people for sharing their memories and impressions: Susan Abramson, Harry Benson, Bill Bohnert, Nancy Cronkite, John Jennings, Quincy Jones, Roger McGuinn, Emily Cole Meisler, John Moffitt, Stephen Moore, Ray Otis, Bob Precht, Peter Prichard, Farris Rookstool III, Don Shaffer, Bob Silverstein, and John Updike.

Thanks to Phyllis Jacobson-Kram for therapeutic and musely duties expertly rendered.

Thanks to my good old friend and fellow Aging Child Robert Aubry Davis for his wise counsel and imagination and to my good new friend Lon Levin for his ideas and inspiration.

Thank you to my brother, Peter Goldsmith, for his indispensable help with the manuscript.

And a million thank-yous to my wife, Amy Roach, for her help, understanding, keen eye, long walks, and tireless support. She loves me, and I know that can't be bad.

Select Bibliography
and Videography

Bibliography

Beatles, The. *The Beatles Anthology.* San Francisco: Chronicle Books, 2000.

Best, Roag, and Pete and Rory Best. *The Beatles: The True Beginnings.* New York: St. Martin's Press, Thomas Dunne Books, 2003.

Bowles, Jerry. *A Thousand Sundays: The Story of the Ed Sullivan Show.* New York: G. P. Putnam's Sons, 1980.

Brown, Peter, and Steven Gaines. *The Love You Make: An Insider's Story of the Beatles.* New York: New American Library, 2002.

Davies, Hunter. *The Beatles: The Authorized Biography.* New York: W. W. Norton & Company, 1996.

Douglas, Susan J. *Where the Girls Are: Growing Up Female with the Mass Media.* New York: Three Rivers Press, 1995.

Everett, Walter. *The Beatles as Musicians: The Quarry Men through Rubber Soul.* Oxford: Oxford University Press, 2001.

Holliday, Johnny, and Stephen Moore. *Johnny Holliday: From Rock to Jock.* Washington: Sports Publishing, 2002.

Kozinn, Allan. *The Beatles.* New York: Phaidon Press, 1995.

Miles, Barry. *The Beatles Diary, Volume 1: The Beatles Years.* London: Omnibus Press, 2001.

Riley, Tim. *Tell Me Why: A Beatles Commentary.* New York: Alfred A. Knopf, 1988.

Sheff, David. *Last Interview: All We Are Saying—John Lennon and Yoko Ono.* London: Sidgwick & Jackson, 2000.

Videography

The Beatles Anthology. (DVD). Apple, 2003.

The Beatles: The First U.S. Visit. (DVD). Apple, 2002.

The Four Ed Sullivan Shows Featuring the Beatles. (DVD). SOFA, 2003.

Index

Abbey Road studios, 77, 78, 81, 83, 87, 92, 98, 179
Adams, Neile, 125
"Ain't She Sweet," 65
Albert, Marsha, 116–17, 118, 124, 150
Allen, Steve, 122
Allerton, 9, 10, 16, 23
"All My Loving," 99, 143, 163
American Bandstand (TV program), 102–3
Anthology (recording), 179
Asher, Jane, 91, 111
Aspinall, Neil, 57, 63, 71, 73, 78, 131, 138
Avalon, Frankie, 130

Bassey, Shirley, 156
BBC, 73, 86, 92
Beat Brothers, 65–66, 70
Beatles haircut, 55, 115, 116, 125, 145, 146, 154, 175
Beatlemania, 61, 92, 95–97, 125–26
Beatles
    American debut, 3, 131–66
    artistry of, 82, 126–27, 168–69, 170, 176–77
    backgrounds of, 1, 8–42, 51–53
    beginnings as group, 36, 39–42, 45, 47, 65, 66, 70, 80, 179–80
    cultural significance of, 3–6, 110–11, 174–75

drummers, 40–41, 45, 78–79, 81
EMI signing of, 76–77
fans' responses to, 85, 86–87, 94–95, 98, 132–33, 135–36, 137, 138–39, 140, 144–45, 154–58, 162, 165, 174
first album, 87–88
first commercial recording, 65–66, 67
first film, 167
"forever young" image of, 179
German-language recordings, 129–30
in Hamburg, 43–59, 63–66, 70, 74–77
"look" and style of, 3, 55, 66, 73–74, 145, 154, 174–75
Martin's influence on, 82–84, 88
media coverage of, 115–16, 145–49, 150, 153–54, 157, 161–62, 165, 172
musical evolution of, 175–77
musicality of, 17, 126–27, 169–70, 175–76
as music industry influence, 169–71
origin of name, 39
recording releases and sales, 167–68, 170–71
youth culture and, 172–74, 177–79
See also individual members

Beatles Fan Club, 74
Beatles for Sale (album), 167
Bedford, Brian, 68, 90
Benson, Harry, 131–32, 133, 164
Bernstein, Sid, 119–20, 124, 155–56
Berry, Chuck, 48, 92, 99, 116, 136
"Besame Mucho," 77
Best, John, 35, 78
Best, Mona, 35, 45, 57, 61, 78–80
Best, Pete, 35, 56, 61, 63, 71, 75, 83
    as Beatles' first drummer, 45, 48,
        49–50, 54, 57–58, 74, 77
    firing of, 78–79, 81
Blackjacks, 45, 57
Block, Ray, 138
Blue album, 89
Bohnert, Bill, 138, 139–40, 143, 162
Bracken, Vivian and James, 102
Brian Poole and the Tremeloes, 72
British Embassy, 151–53
British Invasion, 170
Brown, Georgia, 143–44
Burke, Rodney, 92
Butler, R. A., 153
Butlin's Holiday Camp, 53, 131
Bye Bye Birdie (musical), 137
Byrds, 168, 169
Byrne, John, 51

Caldwell, Alan, 51
Caldwell, Louise Harrison, 28, 114,
    137
Candlestick Park, 168
Cannell, Bud, 114
"Can't Buy Me Love," 167
Capitol Records, 101, 102, 117–19,
    121, 124–25, 130, 148, 159,
    163
Carnegie Hall, 120, 121, 124,
    155–57
Casals, Pablo, 104–5
Casbah Coffee Club, 35, 38, 41, 45,
    57, 58, 63, 70, 73, 78, 179
Cass and the Casanovas, 40, 41

Casser, Brian, 40
Cavern Club, 2, 61–63, 69, 70, 71,
    73, 74, 78, 80, 85, 86, 91, 129,
    179
CBS Evening News (TV program),
    116
CBS television, 109, 121, 124, 136,
    138, 141, 144, 146, 162
Cellarful of Noise, A (Epstein), 69
Charles, Ray, 49, 119
Chiffons, 151
Christian fundamentalists, 171–72
Clapton, Eric, 170
Clark, Dick, 102
classical music, 104–5, 127, 139,
    155, 177–78
Clay, Cassius, 163, 164
Cleave, Maureen, 171
Coasters, 159
Cochran, Eddie, 23
Cohen, Myron, 163
Coleman, Sid, 76
"Come Go with Me," 22
Crickets, 39
Cronkite, Nancy, 139, 145
Cronkite, Walter, 136, 139
"Cry for a Shadow," 65

Davis, Rob, 21
"Day in the Life, A," 175
Deauville Hotel, 124, 158, 160–64
Decca records, 71–72, 73, 75, 76,
    77
Del-Vikings, 22
Demmler, Otto, 130
Derry and the Seniors, 41, 45, 47,
    51
Dexter, Dave, 101, 102, 118, 148
Dick and Dee-Dee, 169
Dicky Doo and the Don'ts, 102
Dixie Cups, 169
"Dominique," 123
Domino, Fats, 48, 58, 119
Donegan, Lonnie, 19–20

"Don't Bother Me," 99
Douglas, Susan, 145–46
Douglas-Home, Alec, 96
"Do You Want to Know a Secret?," 88
"Dream Baby," 73
drugs, 49, 175, 176
Dykins, Robert ("Twitchy"), 18, 25
Dylan, Bob, 169, 174

Eckhorn, Peter, 55, 56, 64
Eddie Clayton Skiffle Group, 53
Ed Sullivan Show (TV program), 121–22, 171
  Beatles' first appearance, 3, 124, 136, 138–48, 178, 183
  Beatles' second appearance, 124, 158, 159, 160–64, 165
  Beatles' third appearance, 124
  spectacular ratings of, 147, 171
"Eleanor Rigby," 182
Eliot, T. S., 4
EMI records, 73, 76, 82, 89, 102
  Beatles signing with, 76–77
  German division, 130
  See also Capitol Records
Epstein, Brian
  background, 67–70
  and Beatles' American tour, 119–24, 130, 131, 140, 149, 153, 160
  as Beatles manager, 74, 78, 81, 84, 118
  and early Beatles recordings, 70–72, 73, 75–77, 78
  homosexuality of, 67, 68, 91
Evans, Mal, 131
Everly Brothers, 48

Faith, Adam, 130
Faron's Flamingos, 41
female fans, 86–87, 95, 144–46, 156, 165
feminism, 145

Fenniman, George, 162
Flaming Pie, 39
Freeman, Robert, 99, 125
"From Me to You," 89, 97, 101, 102, 163
Frost, Robert, 106–7, 109

Gaye, Marvin, 136
Gaynor, Mitzi, 163
General Artists Corporation, 119
Gentle, Johnny, 40, 48
George Martin and the Four Tune Tellers, 76
Germany, 129–30
  Beatles' expulsion from, 56–57
  See also Hamburg
Gerry and the Pacemakers, 41, 63, 73, 83, 170
Goldwater, Barry, 148, 173
Goons, 76
Gorshin, Frank, 144
Gould, Jack, 146
Grade, Lew and Leslie, 122, 123
Graham, Billy, 147–48
Graves, Harry, 52
Guildhall School, 76

Hamburg, 4, 43–59, 80, 83, 85, 90, 99, 129, 151, 176, 179
  and Beatles' development, 42, 58–59, 129
  Beatles' return to, 63–66, 70
  Beatles' third visit to, 74–77
  Liverpool compared with, 44, 57
Hanson, Colin, 21
Hantoon, Colin, 32
Hard Day's Night, A (album), 167
Hard Day's Night, A (film), 129, 153, 167
Harrison, Bernie, 146–47
Harrison, George, 28–36, 114, 178
  background and youth, 28–42
  on Best's firing, 79, 80
  friendship with Paul, 29–30

Harrison, George *(continued)*
  and Quarry Men, 28, 30–36
  song by, 99
  on U.S. trip, 165
  See also Beatles
Harrison, Harold (father), 28, 29, 34
Harrison, Louise (mother), 28–31, 34
Harry, Bill, 67
Haydn, Franz Joseph, 59
"Heartbreak Hotel," 20
Hendrix, Jimi, 170
Herblock (cartoonist), 148
"Here Comes My Baby," 72
hippies, 175
Hollies, 170
Holly, Buddy, 32, 36, 39, 48, 58
Hopkins, Lightnin', 53
Horn, John, 146
Housman, A. E., 179
"How Do You Do It?," 77, 81, 82, 83
Hutchinson, Johnny, 40

Indra (Hamburg club), 47–50, 85
"In Spite of All the Danger," 32
"I Saw Her Standing There," 32, 88, 118, 144, 163
Isley Brothers, 88
"It Won't Be Long," 99
"I Want to Hold Your Hand," 101, 117–18, 120, 125, 126, 129, 144, 148, 150, 163, 167
  analysis of, 111–14
  German-language version, 130

Jacaranda (Liverpool club), 33, 37, 40, 41
James, Carroll ("CJ the DJ"), 116–17, 118, 124, 150
Jay and the Americans, 151
Joel, Billy, 180
John Lennon Airport (Liverpool), 179

Johnny and the Moondogs, 36, 80
Johnson, Lyndon, 172, 173
Jones, Quincy, 131
Joplin, Janis, 170
Justis, Bill, 30

Kaempfert, Bert, 65
Kaiserkeller (Hamburg), 47, 50–51, 53–55, 64
Kaps, Fred, 143
Kaufman, Murray. *See* Murray the K
Kendrick, Alexander, 116
Kennedy, John F., 5, 103–10, 133
  assassination of, 2–3, 100, 107–10, 113
Kennedy, Robert F., 155
Kiley, Tim, 143
Kingsize Taylor and the Dominoes, 63, 79
Kirchherr, Astrid, 54–57, 66, 75, 99
Koschmider, Bruno, 45, 47–51, 53, 56, 64
KXOK (radio station), 113–14, 126

Laurent, Lawrence, 147
Leadbelly, 19
Lee Curtis and the All Stars, 41, 83
Lennon, Cynthia Powell (wife), 80–81, 90, 131, 149
Lennon, Fred (father), 12, 13, 14, 15, 28
Lennon, Jack (grandfather), 12
Lennon, John, 1, 11–36, 179
  background and youth, 1, 11–26, 31–42
  and Beatles' first tour, 39–42
  on Best's firing, 79
  and British Embassy event, 152–53
  and Christian fundamentalists, 171–72
  collaboration with Paul, 11, 24, 27, 31–32, 34, 66, 88, 93, 111–14, 174

effect of mother's death on, 25, 26, 27–28
Epstein's love for, 91
first band. *See* Quarry Men
first meeting with Paul, 4, 7–8, 21–26, 181
on Hamburg experience, 59
on "I Want to Hold Your Hand," 111
literary influences on, 14–15
marriage and birth of son, 80–81, 90
on origin of name "Beatles," 39
personality of, 11
and press conference, 133–35
and Sutcliffe's death, 75
on "Twist and Shout" vocal, 88
See also Beatles
Lennon, Julian (son), 81, 90
Lennon, Julia Stanley (mother), 12–15, 18–20, 25, 26, 37
Lester, Richard, 167
Let It Be (album), 72
"Let It Be" (song), 9
Lewis, Jerry Lee, 22, 169
Liston, Sonny, 163, 164
Litherland Town Hall, 41, 58, 75
Little Anthony and the Imperials, 151
Little Richard, 23, 48, 57, 58, 83
Liverpool, 80, 82, 85, 86, 95, 119, 129
   Beatles landmarks, 1–2, 3, 5–6, 16, 29, 179, 181–82
   Beatles' background in, 8–9, 14, 15, 51–55, 92
   Beatles' return from Hamburg to, 57–59
   Beatles' last Cavern concert in, 91
   Beatles' success in, 61–63, 69–71, 73, 74, 77–78
   Hamburg compared with, 44, 57
Liverpool Art College, 19, 24, 33, 67
Liverpool Institute, 29, 33, 40

Liverpool Oratorio (McCartney), 8–9
Livingston, Alan, 118, 124, 148
Lockwood, Joseph, 76
London, 71, 96
London Palladium, 94–95, 96, 121, 123
"Long Tall Sally," 23, 57, 151
Look Back in Anger (Osborne), 17–18
Lopez, Trini, 129
"Love Me Do," 19, 32, 77, 81, 82, 83, 84
Lowe, John ("Duff"), 32, 33, 36
Lynne, Donna, 151

Maguire, Marie, 52
Mann, William, 126–27
Martin, George, 81, 82, 87, 93, 97, 130, 170
   as Beatles' influence, 82–84, 88
   and Beatles' recordings, 76, 77, 78, 129–30
   and Beatles' U.S. tour, 101, 118, 160
Martin, Judith, 152
Matthew, Brian, 86
McBean, Angus, 89
McCall and Brill, 144
McCartney, Jim (father), 9–11, 31, 32, 34, 71, 93
McCartney, Mary (mother), 9–11, 24
McCartney, Michael (brother), 9, 11
McCartney, Paul, 178
   background and youth, 9–11, 31–42
   on Beatles' career development, 85
   collaboration with John, 11, 24, 27, 31–32, 34, 66, 88, 93, 111–14, 174
   on Epstein as manager, 71
   first meeting with John, 4, 7–8, 21–26, 181
   friendship with George, 29–30

McCartney, Paul *(continued)*
  oratorios by, 8–9, 178
  personality of, 11
  post-Beatles albums by, 39
  and Quarry Men, 33, 36, 37–38
  See also Beatles
McFall, Ray, 62
McGuinn, Roger, 168
Medley, Phil, 88
Meet the Beatles (album), 125, 137
Meisler, Emily Cole, 136–37, 138
"Memphis, Tennessee," 73
Mersey Beat (newsletter), 67, 69, 73
Miami, Fla., 124, 157–65
Milligan, Spike, 76
Minow, Newton, 3–4
Mitchell, Clifford E., 158
Moffitt, John, 138, 140, 165–66
"Money (That's What I Want)," 99
Monkees, 169
Montez, Chris, 86
Moore, Tommy, 40–41
Motown, 98, 102
Murray, Mitch, 77, 81
Murray the K, 132, 136, 149
"My Bonnie Lies Over the Ocean," 65, 66, 69, 70
"My Boyfriend Has a Beatle Haircut," 151

Newby, Chas, 57
Newley, Anthony, 68, 69
Newsweek, 115–16
New York, 135–38, 148, 154–57
North End Music Stores (NEMS), 68, 78

"Octopus's Garden," 182
Oliver! (musical), 143–44
Olympia Theater (Paris), 129
Orbison, Roy, 82, 86, 90
Ormsby-Gore, David, 152
Osborne, John, 17–18
O'Shea, Tessie, 144

Paar, Jack, 131
Paris, 129–30, 131, 132
Parker, Colonel Tom, 141
Parlophone (EMI division), 76
Parnes, Larry, 39–40, 41
Pathé Marconi Studios, 129
Penniman, Richard Wayne. *See* Little Richard
Penny Lane (Liverpool), 2, 16, 29
People and Places (TV program), 86
Phillips, Sam, 30
Plaza Hotel, 135–36, 137, 148, 154, 155
"Please Mr. Postman," 73, 99
Please Please Me (album), 88–89, 98, 100, 167
"Please Please Me" (song), 82–83, 84, 86, 101, 102
Pobjoy, Mr. (headmaster), 18–19
Polydor Records, 65, 66, 69
"Pop Goes the Weasel," 92
Pop Go the Beatles (radio program), 92
Pops and Lenny (TV program), 86
Precht, Bob, 123–24, 138, 139
Presley, Elvis, 20, 122, 141, 145, 169, 170, 172
Prichard, Peter, 122–23, 131
"P.S. I Love You," 77, 81, 82, 83

Quarry Bank High School, 16, 18, 36, 59
Quarry Men, 21–25, 28, 30–39, 80, 181
  name change, 39

Rabbit, Johnny, 126
radio, 73, 85, 86, 92, 177–78
  Beatles' influence on, 170–71
  and Beatles' American debut, 132, 139, 150
  as showcase for Beatles' records, 113–14, 116–17, 125–26, 136
"Raunchy," 30

recording industry, 87–88, 168, 170–71
Red album, 89
Renick, Ralph, 141
Richard, Cliff, 130
Rigby, Eleanor, 181
Rockefeller, Mrs. Nelson, 156–57
"Rock Island Line," 19
rock journalism, 171
rock 'n' roll, 19–20, 28, 35, 37, 53, 88, 177
  Beatles' impact on, 169–70
Rodgers, Richard, 7, 164
Roe, Tommy, 86, 151
Rolling Stones, 170
"Roll Over Beethoven," 99, 116, 151
Ronettes, 131
Rory Storm and the Hurricanes, 41, 51, 53, 54, 63, 83, 131
Rowe, Dick, 72
Royal Command Performance, 97–98, 115, 121, 123, 163
Rusk, Dean, 172–73
Russell, Bert, 88

St. Peter's Church Field, 7, 21, 181–82
Santana, Carlos, 170
Saturday Club (radio program), 86
Secombe, Harry, 76, 97
Sedaka, Neil, 169
Sellers, Peter, 75
Sgt. Pepper's Lonely Hearts Club Band (album), 80, 175
Shacove, Gene, 125
Shaffer, Don ("Stinky"), 113–14, 126
Shannon, Del, 169
Shapiro, Helen, 84, 86, 89, 90
Shea Stadium, 170
Shelley, Percy Bysshe, 4
"She Loves You," 92–94, 97, 99, 101, 102–3, 116, 126, 143, 163, 167

German-language version, 130
Sheridan, Tony, 55, 64, 65, 66, 67
Shirelles, 88, 136
Shotton, Pete, 21, 23
"Silence Is Golden," 72
Silver Beatles, 40–42, 45, 47, 80
Sinatra, Frank, 65, 69, 87, 169, 171, 172
Singing Nun, 122, 141
skiffle music, 19–20, 22, 28, 34, 52–53, 94
Smith, George Toogood (John's uncle), 13, 14, 16, 181
Smith, Mike, 71, 72, 77
Smith, Mimi (John's aunt), 13–16, 18, 19, 20, 25, 31, 57, 81
Sommerville, Brian, 131
Spector, Phil, 131
Standing Stone (McCartney oratorio), 9
Star Club (Hamburg), 74, 77, 83
Starkey, Elsie Gleave, 51, 52
Starkey, Richard, Jr. See Starr, Ringo
Starkey, Richard, Sr., 51
Starr, Ringo, 178
  background and youth, 51–53
  Beatles connection, 53–54, 78, 79, 81–82
  on U.S. trip, 166
  See also Beatles
Stills, Stephen, 170
Stokowski, Leopold, 157
"Strangers in the Night," 65
Strawberry Field, 1–2, 5, 14, 15, 19
"Strawberry Fields Forever," 15
Sullivan, Ed, 119, 161, 162, 163, 164
  and Beatles' American debut, 96, 121–24, 131, 139–42, 144
  See also Ed Sullivan Show
Sunday Night at the London Palladium (TV program), 94–95, 123
Sun Records, 30

Sutcliffe, Stuart, 37–41, 45, 50, 53, 58, 67
  death of, 75
  Varney love affair, 55, 56, 66
Swan Records, 102, 118, 119
Swedish tour, 95, 98, 123
Swinging Blue Jeans, 42, 63

Taylor, Alistair, 70
Teenagers Turn—Here We Go (radio program), 73
television, 3–4, 85, 86, 94
"Thank You Girl," 89
Thank Your Lucky Stars (TV program), 86
"That'll Be the Day," 32
"Think It Over," 36
"This Boy," 118, 163
Tibetan Book of the Dead, 176
"Till There Was You," 72, 98, 143
Toast of the Town (TV show), 121
Topo Gigio, 122, 141
Top Ten Club (Hamburg), 55–56, 63, 64, 65, 66
Tucker, Sophie, 98, 163
"Tutti Frutti," 23
"Twenty Flight Rock," 23
"Twist and Shout," 88, 94, 98, 167

Uline, Miguel, 150
Updike, John, 5

Vartan, Sylvie, 129
Vaughan, Ivan, 21, 22
Vee, Bobby, 169
Vee-Jay Records, 101–2, 118, 119
Vietnam War, 172–73
Vincent, Gene, 48, 58, 75
Vinton, Bobby, 169
Voorman, Klaus, 54, 55, 90

WABC (radio station), 132
Washington, D.C., 149–54
Washington Coliseum, 150–51, 152, 172
Waste Land, The (Eliot), 4
WFUN (radio station), 158
"What'd I Say?," 49
"What Songs the Beatles Sang" (Mann), 126–27
"When I'm Sixty-Four," 32, 182
"When the Saints Go Marching In," 65, 66
Where the Girls Are (Douglas), 145–46
White, Andy, 81
"White Album," 168, 180
Who, 170
"Whole Lotta Shakin' Goin' On," 22
Williams, Allan, 40, 41, 50, 51
  as Beatles manager, 44–45, 46, 56, 64, 70
Willson, Meredith, 72
Wilson, Jo, 117
WINS (radio station), 132, 136
With the Beatles (album), 98–101, 125
WMCA (radio station), 132, 139
WNYC (radio station), 155
Wolfe, Tom, 135–36
"Wonderland by Night," 65
"Wooden Heart," 62
Wooler, Bob, 91
Woolton, 7–8, 13, 21–22, 181
World War II, 8–9, 44
WQAM (radio station), 158
WQXR (radio station), 139
WWDC (radio station), 116–17, 150

"You Really Got a Hold on Me," 99
youth culture, 173–75, 177–79